Clean Ruby

A Guide to Crafting Better Code for Rubyists

Carleton DiLeo

Apress®

Clean Ruby: A Guide to Crafting Better Code for Rubyists

Carleton DiLeo
Boulder, CO, USA

ISBN-13 (pbk): 978-1-4842-5545-2   ISBN-13 (electronic): 978-1-4842-5546-9
https://doi.org/10.1007/978-1-4842-5546-9

Managing Director, Apress Media LLC: Welmoed Spahr
Acquisitions Editor: Steve Anglin
Development Editor: Matthew Moodie
Coordinating Editor: Mark Powers

Cover designed by eStudioCalamar

Cover image designed by Freepik (www.freepik.com)

Distributed to the book trade worldwide by Springer Science+Business Media New York, 233 Spring Street, 6th Floor, New York, NY 10013. Phone 1-800-SPRINGER, fax (201) 348-4505, e-mail orders-ny@springer-sbm.com, or visit www.springeronline.com. Apress Media, LLC is a California LLC and the sole member (owner) is Springer Science + Business Media Finance Inc (SSBM Finance Inc). SSBM Finance Inc is a **Delaware** corporation.

For information on translations, please e-mail editorial@apress.com; for reprint, paperback, or audio rights, please email bookpermissions@springernature.com.

Apress titles may be purchased in bulk for academic, corporate, or promotional use. eBook versions and licenses are also available for most titles. For more information, reference our Print and eBook Bulk Sales web page at http://www.apress.com/bulk-sales.

Any source code or other supplementary material referenced by the author in this book is available to readers on GitHub via the book's product page, located at www.apress.com/9781484255452. For more detailed information, please visit http://www.apress.com/source-code.

Printed on acid-free paper

Table of Contents

About the Author

Carleton DiLeo has been writing code ever since he built his first computer from parts in a dumpster. He has written code for high-traffic web sites to backend big data system to video games. This wide base of knowledge provides Carleton with a unique perspective when writing Ruby code.

Foreword

I have wanted to create software from the moment I first used a computer. The PC was so magical. Armed with a keyboard, I had access to a new digital world with endless possibilities. Not owning a PC, I got access to a computer by riding my bike for miles to a library, or convincing my relatives to let me poke around on their computers. This wasn't enough, I had to have my own. Using parts scavenged from dumpsters in my hometown, I built myself a computer. My greatest find by far was a 500 MB hard drive I stumbled upon in the woods. Taking a walk, I spotted a trail of magnetic tape leading into the bushes, which I followed. At the end, I discovered a hard drive lying there. When I plugged it into my computer, it worked!

After my "new" PC was operational, I spent nights in my bedroom uncovering the secrets it contained. One night, I found a program called QBasic that enabled me to type words into an ugly blue screen and create applications. I was hooked and knew what I wanted to do with my life; in the following years, I read many books to learn more about this new world. Fast-forward over 20 years and the computing landscape looks very different, but the allure is the same.

Who Should Read This Book?

In the past, there were limited options available to become a computer programmer; you went to college and got a degree, or you taught yourself through trial and error. Both required much time and effort. These still exist today, but new boot camp schools keep popping up to satisfy the appetite of a new generation of people hungry to code, with many specializing in Ruby on Rails. They're designed to take a person with little to no coding experience and make them a full-fledged developer in a short period. Quality varies, but they are an excellent way for anyone new to programming to get started; a boot camp provides a sense of direction in a vast ocean of information.

Most students finish a boot camp with a general understanding of programming and skills to create web applications using Ruby on Rails. But few complete the course with the skills needed to craft quality software. There are plenty of resources available that cover this topic in great detail, such as Clean Code[1] and Code Complete[2], but they aren't for Ruby developers. As a mentor for The Firehose Project[3], I referred these books to my students, but found the language barrier was too high. It was too hard to understand the examples or translate ideas to what they spent months learning.

This book is an invaluable guide for developers looking to write good, clean Ruby code. You will learn how to find parts of your code you can improve, and how to start new code the right way. We cover a wide variety of topics; along the way, you will learn how to craft the best variables, methods, modules, and classes. By the time you finish, you'll know what it means to write code that improves productivity and the morale of your team.

---

[1]*Clean Code* by Robert Cecil Martin is an excellent handbook for any developer. Using real-world examples written in Java, Robert demonstrates how to improve code step by step using real-world Java examples.

[2]*Code Complete* by Steve McConnell is the manual for writing better code. It's a monster of a book with every page filled with great tips. Topics are not relevant to Ruby since the examples are C#, Java, and C++. I still recommend it as a great reference.

[3]The Firehose Project is an online boot camp. Students take part weekly in 1-hour sessions with mentors.

CHAPTER 1

The Qualities of Clean Code

So what is clean code? If you ask three different developers, you will get three different answers. It's a hard concept to define. You know clean code when you see it, as if written by a programming wizard from a distant land. We all want to write good code that others admire. Sometimes we don't know where to start. How do we take our messy, unorganized code and turn it into something beautiful?

Many factors determine clean code, but we will focus on these:

- Readable

- Easy to change

- Straightforward

Examine code you've written. How many of those questions can you answer yes? It's unlikely you said yes to all of them. It's more realistic you said no to at least one or more. Even the most experienced developers have a hard time achieving this, so don't worry. The skills required to create clean code take time and patience to learn. As you learn new techniques, try them in your code and pick the ones that work for you. There is trial and error involved, but this book will be your guide along the way.

© Carleton DiLeo 2019
C. DiLeo, *Clean Ruby*, https://doi.org/10.1007/978-1-4842-5546-9_1

Readability

Code readability describes the effort required to understand what a piece of code does. Readable code should be like a well-written book; it doesn't expect you to dig into the details to discover its purpose. It should be easy to understand a variable's meaning, or what a method will do when [^^Invoked]. With unreadable code, you must read multiple times before you get the meaning. After reading unreadable code, you have many questions. You will spend more time understanding it than changing it.

Let's start with a simple code example of code that is *not* readable:

```
1   def method1(t, b)
2     c = t + b
3     return c
4   end
```

Examine the code and ask yourself the following questions:

- Is the code easy to understand?

- What does this code do?

Several design decisions have made this small method hard to read. The method name is ambiguous, and the variable names are vague. These issues prevent us from understanding what the code is trying to do. This example may be extreme, but finding unreadable code like this in the wild is possible. It's OK because with a little effort, this code will be so much better.

Before we continue, let's talk about variables. They are the storage containers of our application, which allow us to keep bits of information in memory for computation. A single application can have thousands of variables, but none should be superfluous. The earlier example has an extra variable, c, which is both nondescript and unnecessary; it decreases the readability of the method because it adds bloat. Code bloat is bad because a developer has to read more code than necessary.

This is how we could rewrite the earlier example:

```
1   def sum(a, b)
2     a + b
3   end
```

This example is much easier to read. It does the same thing, but it has a better method name and better variable names that give clues on the code's intent. The name **sum** tells the reader it will calculate the sum of its parameters, **a** and **b**. The method arguments, **a** and **b**, are short, but descriptive enough in this context. We removed the **c** variable and instead returned the result of our operation to the calling code. Ruby returns the last expression of a method, which means storing the result of a + b in a separate variable is redundant and unnecessary.

What did we accomplish with this refactor? The new method is easy to read and comprehend with little effort. As a result, you spend less energy trying to understand the code and more effort adding new functionality. Next time you are programming, make sure you take the time to proofread what you wrote. Does the code need much effort to understand? Do variable names describe the data they represent and method names inform the reader of their intent? Make sure you don't leave any room for doubt.

Extensibility

Code can change for various reasons: new product requirements, gems need upgrading to fix bugs, and old code gets refactored. As developers, we must adapt because code we are writing now will change. It's important to prepare. The steps we take to make our code *extensible* will pay dividends later.

During my career, I've used shortcuts to "save" time. I've convinced myself there wasn't enough time to do it the right way. I often regretted my decision later. Taking more time to design an extensible solution, I would have produced code that was not so fragile and hard to change. Don't make the same mistakes I've made. Think how your code might change and plan for it.

The following example of a logging method *isn't* extensible:

```
1   def log(message, level)
2     if level.to_s == 'warning'
3       puts "WARN: #{message}"
4     elsif level.to_s == 'error'
5       puts "ERROR: #{message}"
6     end
7   end
8
9   log("An error occurred", :error)
```

This example defines the method **log**, which pre-pends either "WARN" or "ERROR" to the message argument depending on the logging **level**. The method displays the message to the console using **puts**. It's simple and easy to read, but an issue remains.

Let's add another logging level to the **log** method:

```
1   def log(message, level)
2     if level.to_s == 'warning'
3       puts "WARN: #{message}"
4     elsif level.to_s == 'info'
5       puts "INFO: #{message}"
6     elsif level.to_s == 'error'
7       puts "ERROR: #{message}"
8     end
9   end
10
11   log("Something happened", :info)
```

Notice the **elsif** added to handle the new **info** logging level. The change is trivial because the method is short. Imagine adding more logging levels to the **log** method. If left unchecked, each new log level increases complexity until making even trivial changes becomes impossible. This is something we can prevent by designing our code to be extensible.

Here is another example where we changed the **log** method to handle new log levels:

```
1  def log(message, level)
2    puts "#{level.to_s.upcase}: #{message}"
3  end
4
5  log("An error occurred", :error)
```

Instead of an **if/else** statement to control how we format the message, we use built-in Ruby features to simplify the logic. To avoid string literals like "WARN" and "ERROR", we use **String#upcase** to convert the argument **level** from a symbol **:error** to a string "ERROR". Next, we use string interpolation to pre-pend the log level to the message argument.

Not only was a lot of code removed, but adding a new **level** requires zero changes to the log method. This is great because we won't need to touch it again unless we want to add more features. There is little chance to introduce bugs since the method rarely changes, and fewer bugs is always good.

Simplicity

There are many ways to solve a problem. A team of developers can argue for hours on the best approach to solve even the most trivial issue. Clever solutions are designed, often ignoring simple ones. But they are hard to understand, even by the person who created them. It's difficult to create a simple solution. It requires you to stow your ego and be comfortable with building code that is straightforward instead of showing your skill.

The source code for the 1993 game *Doom* by id Software is an excellent example. Video games contain much data that represents level layouts, player stats, and computer graphics. *Doom* was revolutionary on game design, but the developers kept things simple by storing most of the game's data in arrays. After the release of the source code, other developers pointed out how wrong this approach was because other data structures could have performed better. What most of these developers didn't realize is that by using simple data structures, *Doom*'s source code was easy to work with and less error-prone. The simplicity of the code required fewer brain cells to understand. It freed up id Software to focus on pushing the boundaries of game design and not getting tripped up by complexity.

What does simple code look like? Here is an example of code that is *not* simple:

```
1   def log_to_console(args)
2    if args.length > 1
3      if args[1] == 'warn'
4         puts 'WARN: ' + args[0]
5      elsif args[1] == 'error'
6         puts 'ERROR: ' + args[0]
7      else
8         puts args[0]
9      end
10    end
11   end
12
13   args = ['A message', 'warn']
14   log_to_console(args)
```

This method might be familiar because it's like the earlier section. I have added more code that complicates the logic, but the purpose of the method remains the same: print a message with the associated log level to the console. Although it works as intended, we'll now look at a more straightforward approach.

First, we will change the method definition to use two explicit parameters instead of an array.

```ruby
1   def log_to_console(message, level = :info)
2     if level == :warn
3       puts 'WARN: ' + message
4     elsif level == error
5       puts 'ERROR: ' + message
6     else
7       puts message
8     end
9   end
10
11  log_to_console('A message', :warn)
```

Reduce the number of **if** statements.

```ruby
1   def log_to_console(message, level)
2     puts "#{level}: " + message
3   end
4
5   log_to_console('A message', :warn)
```

Use built-in Ruby methods to simplify the code.

```ruby
1   def log_to_console(message, level = :info)
2     puts "#{level.to_s.upcase}: #{message}"
3   end
4
```

```
5   log_to_console('A message', :warn)
6   log_to_console('Another message', :anything_we_want)
7   log_to_console('Another message')
```

There is much less code, but with the same functionality. It's easier to understand how to use it without looking at the internals. We change the method definition, removed the if statements, and used string interpolation instead. If we want another log level, we won't need to add any more code. We leveraged a method on the **String** class to handle capitalizing the log level. We used optional arguments to offer flexibility.

If you want to write clean code, consider simple solutions first. Avoid using complicated solutions unless you can't solve your problem with a simple one. If you still get lost, just remember K.I.S.S or "Keep it simple, stupid."

CHAPTER 2

Naming Things

Coming up with names for the variables, classes, and methods in a program is not an easy task. We must be gurus to think of a name at a moment's notice. It's part of our everyday coding lives, and we can't let down our guard. Choosing the wrong name has significant implications and can determine whether code is easy to read or confusing and cryptic. It doesn't end there, because poor-quality names have a compounding effect. One bad name encourages creating more bad names; those bad names promote even more bad names. Progress crawls to a halt because these bad names make our code impossible to understand.

Why create a bad name? They make our code harder to work with. Nobody wants to make their job harder, but it's not so simple. Most bad names happen due to lack of knowledge and misplaced priorities. Consider the last time you created a variable or method name that didn't make you proud. Most likely you didn't intentionally choose that inferior name. There may have been a deadline to meet, and sacrifices were needed.

How do we avoid being caught in these situations? First you must understand that the time spent creating a good class, method, or variable name is worth it. Don't wait until later to choose a better name because it never comes, and there will always be something more pressing.

The second step is to acquire the knowledge needed to make informed decisions. Knowledge is a programmer's best friend. Without it, we must guess and assume, but computers don't understand assumptions. They need us to give exact commands to work. It's essential we know the systems

© Carleton DiLeo 2019
C. DiLeo, *Clean Ruby*, https://doi.org/10.1007/978-1-4842-5546-9_2

we are working with to make informed decisions. Picking names are no different. There are skills and knowledge we can learn to make it easier. It's iterative and that takes time to master, but worth it. Let's get started.

Variables

The first stop on our journey is variable naming. Variables are the building blocks of a Ruby program. Without them, we have nowhere to store data. Since variables play such an essential role in our application, the name you choose will play a fundamental role in creating clean code. Picking a good name allows the reader to understand what data the variable has. A good name takes away the guesswork. There is no risk of the reader making assumptions and making changes that introduce bugs.

There is much to consider when selecting variable names, with length and word types playing a crucial role. Avoid pitfalls that make our names ambiguous. The most important thing is to trust your instincts. Sometimes, a developer will pick a good name only to second-guess themselves and change it to something of lesser quality.

Naming Conventions

Coding conventions are guidelines for developers to follow. They make it possible for a team to write code using a single voice, as if written by a single developer. Naming conventions make variable names consistent. This is important because constantly changing variable formats makes code confusing. Your team should pick a naming convention and stick with it. Just imagine if you visited a place where everyone spoke a different dialect of the same language. After the second or third dialect change, your brain would be struggling to understand.

Consider the pros and cons of each variable naming convention. No matter which one you pick, don't change it after you've written code. It's better to have a suboptimal naming convention than multiple. Let's examine some variations.

Hungarian Notation

Most programming languages have a preferred convention based on the language's strengths and weaknesses. Code from an application written in the C programming language will most likely use Hungarian notation.

Look at this example:

```
1    # Example of Hungarian notation in C
2    int iUserId = 1;
```

Notice the **i** pre-pended to the variable name **UserId**. This extra prefix character **i** is a hint to the data stored in the variable, informing us that the type is an integer. The added information can be useful in a C program where data is passed between functions. Knowing the variable data type saves us time. We won't need to go digging to find the original variable definition, since the variable has the information we need.

These advantages might sound enticing, but this extra information is overkill for Ruby applications. Providing hints is unnecessary since most variables have a short scope. Locating the original variable definition is not time-consuming. Ruby is an object-oriented programming language with long-lived and complex data encapsulated in a class. Instead of passing argument data from method to method, we can wrap common methods and variables in a class.

Instead of this code:

```
1    def state_tax(total)
2      total * 0.2
3    end
4
```

```
5   def federal_tax(total)
6     total * 0.1
7   end
```

We can do better.

```
1   class Tax
2    def initialize(total)
3      # Total is now an instance variable
4      # and can be accessed by all methods
5      @total = total
6    end
7
8    def state
9      @total * 0.2
10    end
11
12    def federal
13      @total * 0.1
14    end
15   end
```

Ruby is a dynamically typed language, so data types can change at run time. This means a data type hint that was once correct could end up being incorrect if the variable's data type changes. A variable that contained an Integer in one part of our code might be a string somewhere else. I'm not recommending you write your code this way. I just want you to be aware of the possibility.

Pre-pending more information can be detrimental to the reader. When reading a variable name that uses Hungarian notation, our brain has to comprehend what **i** means every time. This may be inconsequential, but when you're reading hundreds or thousands of lines of code, it requires more brain cycles. Every time you read the variable name, you will ask yourself "What does **i** mean? Does it mean *index* or *integer* or maybe something else?" It's easy to get fatigued by the added work. Programming is taxing mentally, so let's not make it any harder.

Camel Case

The camel case naming convention is popular among curly bracket languages such as Java, C++, and C#. This convention capitalizes the first letter of each word in a variable, so it resembles humps on a camel's back.

```
1   # All words capitalized. Good for public properties.
2   int UserId = 1;
3
4   # Capitalize starting with second word. Good for local or
        private variables.
5   int userId = 1;
```

Camel casing has two different variants. The first variant capitalizes the first letter of every word, and the second variant capitalizes every word after the first word. Combining the first and second variants can offer visual cues on variable scope.

Ruby doesn't allow variable names to start with an uppercase letter. We can use camel case, but can only use the variant which capitalizes words in a variable name beginning with the second word.

Snake Case

The final naming convention we will cover is snake case, the preferred convention for Ruby programs. It separates each word of a variable name with an underscore.

```
1   user_id = 1
```

It doesn't have the constraints we saw with camel case and doesn't clutter the code with unnecessary information as Hungarian notation. You should use snake case, unless you have a good reason. If you're working in a codebase that has an established naming convention, switching to snake case convention might be more work than it's worth. It's more important to be consistent then pick the perfect naming convention.

The Data

When choosing a variable name, it's critical to understand the contained value. We often overlook this when creating names, and most good names are obvious. For example, say we have a variable that stores the _number of steps_ needed to complete a process. There are many names we could select, but the underlined phrase is exact. The name _number_of_steps_ tells readers what data the variable contains. We could add more words to improve accuracy, but that makes our name too long. Besides, the variable will be inside a method or class that gives more information. If the variable **number_of_steps** was located in the method **start()** that was in the class **Process**, a developer could assume the variable **number_of_steps** is the number of steps of a process.

Look at these examples:

```
1    # Bad example
2    user = 'bob'
3
4    # Good example
5    first_name = 'bob'
```

In the "bad" example, we have the variable **user** which should contain a user. Upon closer inspection, we see that the variable has the first name of a user. The variable name **user** doesn't tell the reader enough. Readers understand that the variable has **user** data, but they won't know it is the user's first name. Also **user** is misleading since the reader might think it's an instance of the **User** class.

In the "good" example, we change the variable name to **first_name** to be more specific. Our new name doesn't tell the reader that **first_name** has a user's first name, but that's okay. Method and class names should offer more context. If for whatever reason the method or class name doesn't help, then we need to change the variable name to give more context. Since the variable has the first name of a user, we might pre-pend the word *user*. We get **user_first_name**, which is longer but clear.

Here is one more example.

```
1    # Bad example
2    start_data = { players: 4, score_to_win: 5 }
3
4    # Good example
5    game_config = { players: 4, score_to_win: 5 }
```

The next example is more complicated since the "bad" example has a hash variable **start_data** with data for a game. The reader assumes it is used when the application starts, but doesn't know the purpose. Only through closer examination, do they realize that the hash defines the configuration of a game.

In the "good" example, we change the name to something more descriptive. The new name, **game_config**, tells the reader that the hash is a game configuration. This is better because it provides more information about the value, and the name is explicit without being too wordy. The name **game_config** is flexible enough to allow new hash keys without requiring us to change to the variable name. As long as any new hash key is a game configuration, we are good.

Length

When we name a variable, we want that name to be as descriptive as possible. A descriptive name allows the reader to understand your intent without having to spend time reading other parts of your code. Be careful since it's possible for a name to be too descriptive. When variable names grow too long, it becomes hard for the eyes to follow, more difficult to understand, and readers get lost. For comparison, a long variable name is similar to a run-on sentence in a book. The reader has to keep information in their head while trying to comprehend the sentence. Understanding its meaning becomes difficult the longer the sentence is. Short descriptive sentences are easier to digest. Our variables should follow the same guidelines: be short and to the point. Remember, less code is easier to read than tons of code.

One of the first things you can do to keep your variable names short is to avoid adding unnecessary information. It's okay to leave out words if the reader can still interpret the meaning. We want our variable names to read like English, but it's okay to be broken English. Most people reading your code will be smart enough to figure out what you meant with little effort.

Avoid storing too much data in a single variable. It's easy to create names that are too long because we want to share so much information. Breaking a single variable into multiple variables can simplify your code and make it much easier to follow.

These are more examples.

```
1   # Bad example
2   purchase_final_sale_total = 300
3
4   # Good example
5   sale_total = 300
```

The "bad" example is hard to read at first glance because of its length, and not easy to understand how it's used. There are just too many words. We need to figure out what each word means in context of the others.

Now look at the "good" example, where we simplified the name greatly by removing words. The new variable name is only two words, but these two words give enough information to communicate what data the variable is storing. The extra words from the original name, purchase and final, were redundant. These words add nothing to the reader's understanding of the variable. Removing these words doesn't take away anything and adds clarity.

Avoid Unnecessary Information

A common pitfall for most developers when naming variables is relying on naming crutches. A developer will add extra words to the beginning or end of a variable name to help readers understand the contents. The problem is, these words end up diluting the clarity of the name. They are useless additions that do more harm than good. Usually an alternate name could be more descriptive.

Naming Crutches

Naming crutches are easy to spot, starting with this small list. Knowing these words will make it easy to locate other similar crutches.

- Manager

- Data

- Info

- List

Although not exhaustive, you should get the idea. These types of words are generic and hurt reader understanding of the variable. In the next example, we include the class name as part of our discussion of variable names. The ideas discussed for class names very much apply to variable names.

```
1    # Bad example
2    class PlayerManager
3      def spawn(player_id)
4        @players << Player.new(player_id)
5      end
6    end
7
8    player_manager = PlayerManager.new
9    player_manager.spawn(1)
```

In this example, we have the class **PlayerManager** that we instantiate
and store in a variable named **player_manager**. This combines the two
words of player and manager, where "manager" implies it's managing
something and "player" indicates players. The problem with this name is
the word "manage" can mean many things. Is the PlayerManager going to
manage a player's location, or their stats?

Having the word *manager* added to the end of a variable or class name
creates ambiguity. The reader won't know its responsibility. This confusion
might cause them to misuse your variable, or think it's okay to add just
about anything. The class will become a super class[1] and be a constant
sore spot in your codebase.

Change the names to be more descriptive. If the class only handles
player spawning, then the name should show that. When we create a
variable or class, we should pick a name that is simple and describes what
the class does now. Don't be a fortune teller and predict the future. We
can always create more variables and classes to fulfill future requirements.
Let's look at how we might change the example to drop the word *manager*
from the variable and class name.

---

[1]Super classes are classes with the most lines of code in your entire
application. They try to do everything for a concept and are extremely hard to
support. Any other classes that need these methods can do the same thing.

```
1   # Good example
2   class PlayerSpawner
3     def spawn(player_id)
4       @players << Player.new(player_id)
5     end
6   end
7
8   player_spawner = PlayerSpawner.new
9   player_spawner.spawn(1)
```

We changed our class and variable names from **PlayerManager** and **player_manager** to **PlayerSpawner** and **player_spawner**. This clarifies that the **PlayerSpawner** class handles player spawning, and the **player_spawner** variable is an instance of this class. The role of these two elements is described in their names.

What if we plan to add more functionality? Say we want **PlayerSpawner** to handle scoring. If the class was named **PlayerManager**, adding logic to manage player scores makes sense. Since we changed our code to follow the Single Responsibility Principle[2], adding scoring logic makes little sense. We would need to create a new class that handles this role. A class name like **PlayerScore** fits this responsibility.

Avoid Conjunctions

Using conjunctions in your variable names shows we are attempting to store too much data in a single variable. The English language defines conjunction as a word (e.g., words like **and**, **or**, **but**) that connects two clauses into the single phrase. If you spot a conjunction in a variable name,

---

[2]Single Responsibility Principle is a concept that dictates our code should only be responsible for one thing.

it should raise a red flag that something is wrong. Let's look at an example where a variable uses a conjunction.

```
1    # Bad example
2    score_and_player_count = { score: 100, player_count: 2 }
```

Here we have a variable that contains a hash with two data points: current score and player count. While the name **score_and_player_count** is descriptive, the word "and" shows that the variable is holding data for two different purposes. This means we are trying to do too much with one variable which will lead to problems.

If we added more key/value pairs to the hash, the variable name might need to change, so it continues to describe the data. Changing a variable name because its data changed is bad. If the variable name changes, any places in the code that references the variable will need to change. This workflow will lead to bugs and extra work.

Also, as the variable name grows in size, it will become harder to read. Let's look at a better approach.

```
1    # Good example
2    score = 100
3    player_count = 2
```

Here we split our single variable into two. Each variable only holds a single data point, and the names show this. Both variables are short and easy to read. Now that each variable holds a specific data point, future developers will be less likely to append unrelated data to it. Since the variables contain precise data, it's also unlikely we will need to change the name.

Only Alpha Characters

We want to avoid numeric characters in our variable names, if possible. Using a number often detracts from the variable's meaning, and usually there is a better way. This is an example of two different variables that hold the same data.

```
1    # Bad example
2    year_1985 = '1985'
3
4    # Good example
5    start_of_grunge = '1985'
```

The variable in the "bad" example informs the reader it has the year *1985*. This is correct, but it doesn't tell us what the year 1985 means to the code. Also, if the value of the variable changes to anything besides 1985, then the name will be misleading. The variable name **start_of_grunge** in the "good" example tells us what the year 1985 represents. If we need to change the year to 1986, the variable name can stay the same because it reflects what the data represents and not the data itself.

Tracking versions is a special case that might justify having numbers in your variable name. It would be reasonable to store the first version of something in a variable named **version1** and the second version in **version2**. Use your best judgment in situations like this. Decide if having the numeric character in your variable name is necessary.

Methods

Methods are the building blocks of reusable code. Without them, we would have to copy and paste the same code repeatably. It's vital that our methods give hints about what they do. Vague or incorrect method names can confuse. Confusion can cause headaches for other developers and bugs in our code. Let's look at some techniques you can use to avoid this.

Use Verbs

Methods are the doers of our application. They authenticate users for a web application and send emails to customers after they made a purchase. Methods contain the behavior that makes our software what it is. Since methods perform the actions in our application, we should use verbs to name them.

Our code should read like a phrase or a sentence in a book. Creating method names that are the inverse of a well-written sentence can make our code hard to read. How do you converse with other people? Telling a coworker "I'm going to **money** the customer's account" would be confusing. This is because we used a noun instead of a verb to describe an action. If you said "I'm going to **bill** the customer's account," then your coworker would know you will send a customer a bill. These rules apply to method naming. Look at this example:

```
1   class Account
2     def initialize(customer)
3       @customer = customer
4     end
5
6     # Bad method
7     def money(amount)
8       @customer.balance -= amount
9     end
10  end
```

Here we used the noun **money** for our method name, but that only provides context without telling what it's doing with the money. It's possible to guess that it will add or subtract the amount from the customer's account but it's unclear. Now let's change the method to use a verb.

```
1   class Account
2     def initialize(customer)
3       @customer = customer
4     end
5
6     # Good method
7     def pay_bill(amount)
8       @customer.balance -= amount
9     end
10  end
```

Now the method name has the verb **pay**. The word **pay** tells the reader the action the method will perform. Paired with the noun **bill**, we know that intent of the method is to pay a bill. Since this method is part of the **Account** class, we can assume that the method is paying a bill for an account. Let's see another bad and good example in action.

```
1   # Bad Example
2   account = Account.new(current_user)
3   account.money(100)
4
5   # Good Example
6   account = Account.new(current_user)
7   account.pay_bill(100)
```

In the "bad" example, we are creating an instance of **Account**. When we call the **money** method, it's unclear what will happen to the value we passed. In the "good" example, we create an instance of the improved **Account** class. On the next line, we call the **pay_bill** method. It's clear that the value passed to the method will pay a bill.

Return Value

Another item to consider when choosing a name is the data type returned by the method. If the method returns a boolean value, our method should have a question mark appended to the end.

```
1  def equal?(a, b)
2    a == b
3  end
```

In this example, our method takes two values and determines if they are equal. The question mark in the method name shows that the method will return a true or false value. Since we know that the method returns a boolean value, we can use the method like this:

```
1  if equal?('test', 'test')
2    puts 'test is equal to test'
3  end
```

This code checks if the two values are equal using our method and prints a message to the console. The ? tells the reader that the method will cause a true or false result. It's a small, but helpful, addition to our method name.

It's possible to use a *linking verb* instead of a question mark to achieve the same effect.

```
1  # We pre-pended the word is to the method name
2  if is_equal('test', 'test')
3    puts 'test is equal to test'
4  end
```

This code is very readable, but Ruby convention recommends that we use the question instead. Most Ruby developers will use the question mark convention; I suggest you adopt this.

Bang Methods

Bang methods are unique methods that change the data of the called object. You can spot bang methods because they end with a **!**. The exclamation point tells the reader that calling this method is dangerous, and the effects are irreversible. If you create a method that changes the data of an object, mark it with an exclamation point to avoid confusion. Bang methods also exist in the Ruby core library, so it's important to understand how they work.

Find the Array class in your favorite Ruby documentation web site. Notice how methods have versions with and without an exclamation mark. The logic for each method is the same, but one method will make a copy leaving the original data intact, while the other method will change the original array.

Let's see how this looks:

```
1   class User
2     attr_accessor :friends
3
4     def remove_friend!(friend)
5       @friends.delete(friend)
6     end
7   end
```

Here we have a class with a single method. The method **remove_friend!** changes the friends collection (and causing real-life turmoil). The **!** warns the reader of the ramifications of calling this method.

Like we mentioned earlier, Ruby's core library uses this convention. Methods like the **sort** method on the **Array** class have a version that sorts the called instance and another version that returns a sorted copy.

```
1   numbers = [2,3,1]
2   numbers.sort! # <= This will sort the numbers array
3   numbers = [2,3,1]
4   new_numbers = numbers.sort # <= new_numbers will contain
    the sorted copy of numbers
```

Classes

The power of object-oriented programming shines when we group similar data and behavior into classes. Classes make our code easy to comprehend and prevent code duplication. They are the foundation of Ruby applications, so it's important we take care when naming them. Bad class names make even a simple application hard to understand.

Choosing a class name is like choosing a variable name. The name you pick for a class should show the data and behavior it encapsulates. This is not a trivial task though. Finding the right word that describes what your class can take time and many iterations. It's common to change a class name several times before settling on one that fits. In this chapter, we will discuss techniques that will help you find a good name for your classes.

Purpose

Developers don't make classes just for the fun of it. There are many reasons to create a class. Maybe several methods and variables are related, and it made sense to group them into a reusable component. Working on a new feature can create the need for new classes to wrap business logic. While the reason may vary, we create classes to fulfill a purpose. That purpose can be described in a word or phrase.

Let's look at an example where a group methods and data fulfill a common purpose.

```
1    def new_user_add_coins
2      # code
3    end
4
5    def email_new_user_welcome(email)
6      # send an email
7    end
8
9    user_email = 'example@example.com'
10   new_user_add_coins
11   email_new_user_welcome(user_email)
```

Here we have two methods and a variable, acting on behalf of a new user. If you look closer, you see that the variable and method names also repeat the word **new** and **user** many times. When you look at patterns like this where methods or variables pre-pend a familiar word to their name, it's a sign that introducing a new class would help simplify the code.

Now that we identified code that is a good candidate for a new class, we need a name. Before we pick a class name, we need to know its purpose in our application. Both methods being added perform **user setup**. I highlighted the two words **User** and **Setup** because these words offer a good description of what our new class will do. If we combine these two words, it creates a very nice class name, **UserSetup**. Look at the following example, where we define the new class.

```
1    class UserSetup
2      def initialize(user)
3        @user = user
4      end
5
6      def execute
7        add_coins
```

```
 8       send_welcome
 9     end
10
11     private
12     def add_coins
13       # add coins to their account
14     end
15
16     def send_welcome
17       email = @user.email
18       # send an email
19     end
20   end
21
22   user_setup = UserSetup.new(user)
23   user_setup.execute
```

Our new class has a single public method named **execute** that calls two private methods, which should look familiar. They are the two methods from the prior example, but the names have changed. We removed **new_ user_** from **add_coins** and changed **email_new_user_welcome** to **send_ welcome**. Since our class name UserSetup provides context to the purpose of the class, the method names can be shorter and nonspecific. Also, the methods in the class no longer need any arguments because the new class requires a user upon instantiation.

Below the class definition, we created an instance of UserSetup and called the **execute** method. Even in isolation from the class definition, it's easy to understand what these last two lines do. The class name **UserSetup** does a great job informing the reader that the logic in the class handles the setup process for a user. We need not know the specifics of the setup process to use the class.

Role

Some classes perform a particular role. For example, some encapsulate ActiveRecord queries, while others handle requests to external APIs. These types of classes have names that inform the reader of their specific job.

In a Rails application, it's common to see queries like this in a controller class.

```
1    inactive_users = User.where(last_login: 6.months.ago,
     paid_account: false)
```

This query fetches inactive users from a database. The state "inactive" for this example means users have not logged in for six months and are not paying customers. The query itself is simple, but we need to find how to make it easy to test and reuse.

In the next example, we move the query code to a new class:

```
1    class InActiveUserQuery
2      def initialize(relation = User)
3        @relation = relation
4      end
5
6      def all
7        @relation.where(
8          last_login: 6.months.ago,
9          paid_account: false
10       )
11     end
12   end
13
14   inactive_user_query = InActiveUserQuery.new(User)
15   inactive_users = inactive_user_query.all
```

First, we will break the class name into two parts. The first part of the name represents the resource being queried: **InActiveUser**. The second part represents the role the class is performing: **Query**. The class name **InActiveUserQuery** tells readers that this class will query the database for inactive users. Without the word **Query** in our name, the class would look like an ordinary model class. Specifying a role lets readers know what the class can do without having to guess.

The **Query** class is just one of the many types we might create. Other role-specific classes like **Presenter**, **Controller**, and **Helper** offer the same benefit as the Query, but for different roles.

Modules

A module is like a class except you can't instantiate it. Instead, the include keyword injects them into other parts of our code. Why would we create this instead of a class? Modules exist because not everything we code makes sense as a class. Specific concepts are a grouping of shared ideas rather than a concrete object. To show this, the next example defines the class **Math**. It has two methods: **add** and **subtract**.

```
1   class Math
2     def add(a, b)
3       a + b
4     end
5
6     def subtract(a, b)
7       a - b
8     end
9   end
10
11  math = Math.new
12  sum = math.add(2, 2)
```

The class is simple but awkward to use. To use the methods in the class, we need to create an instance of **Math**. This makes little sense because "creating a math" is a nonsensical statement, but that's what the sample is doing. Math is an abstract collection of concepts used to compute numbers, but a class isn't a good fit. Grouping the **add** and **subtract** methods together and making it easy to use in other classes is still desirable. This is where modules come in handy. The next example changes use a module instead of a class.

```
1    module Math
2      def add(a, b)
3        a + b
4      end
5
6      def subtract(a, b)
7        a - b
8      end
9    end
10
11   class CashRegister
12     include Math
13
14     def calculate_change(total_cost, amount_paid)
15       subtract(amount_paid, total_cost)
16     end
17   end
```

Instead of a class, we used a module to encapsulate the two methods. Next, we include it in the class **CashRegister**, which now has access to methods defined in the **Math** module. Any other classes can do the same thing.

When you are thinking about what to name a module, think about what functionality the module is grouping. If you find more than a single concept, split the module into multiple modules until the grouping becomes clear.

CHAPTER 3

Creating Quality Methods

A method is the smallest block of code in an application. Methods can be reused, which helps prevent duplication. A method hides the details of an operation, so refactoring will not affect the calling code. This takes careful planning to achieve. In this chapter, we will discuss different techniques used to create quality methods: parameters, return values, guard clauses, length, comments, and nesting.

Parameters

Without parameters, there would be no way to manipulate method outcome. Parameters make methods flexible, which creates opportunities for reuse and helps prevent code duplication. Instead of copying and altering an existing method to fit a different need, we use a parameter. Less code to write and support saves us time.

Parameters are a valuable addition to our programming toolbox, but they pose a risk. When misused, they increase code complexity and make a method hard to understand. Use caution when introducing parameters to a method.

© Carleton DiLeo 2019
C. DiLeo, *Clean Ruby*, https://doi.org/10.1007/978-1-4842-5546-9_3

Use Fewer Parameters

The more parameters you define for a method, the harder it is to understand and support. Noticing the increased complexity isn't easy when we are dealing with only one or two parameters. The difference in complexity becomes clearer with each added parameter.

This is a method with no parameters:

```
1   def greeting
2     "Hello"
3   end
```

The calling code can't manipulate the method outcome since it will only return the string "Hello".

Let's add one parameter.

```
1   def greeting(name)
2     "Hello #{name}"
3   end
```

We added a single parameter to allow the calling code to specify a name to append after the greeting. This simple addition introduces new things to consider. Since we do not control it, the name being passed to the method can be any of the following values:

- string

- nil

- string with multiple words

The current implementation only considers the first value. A nil value produces less than an optimal return value.

```
1   => "Hello "
```

This return value has extra spaces. We improve the method by calling rstrip to remove any spaces to the right of **Hello**.

```
1    def greeting(name)
2      "Hello #{name}".rstrip
3    end
```

If the calling code passes a nil value, now the method returns "Hello" with no extra spaces.

The other possible value is a string that has multiple words. The method doesn't account for this. If we were to pass the string "Jane is learning Ruby", the result is:

```
1    "Hello Jane is learning Ruby"
```

The return value is okay, but not expected. We need to make a decision how to handle this type of input. The following example is a simple solution that only uses the first word in the string.

```
1    def greeting(name)
2      "Hello #{name.split.first}".rstrip
3    end
```

This splits the name parameter into an array of string values. By default, the split method uses a space to split the string. The string "Jane is learning Ruby" from the earlier example will become an array of four words: ["Jane", "is", "learning", "Ruby"]. Next, we pick the first element of the array, "Jane".

Now the method returns the following string:

```
1    "Hello Jane"
```

Our return value looks better. We could continue to poke holes in the **greeting** method, but adding one additional parameter introduced complexity. Imagine adding another one to specify whether the greeting is formal or informal. You will need to consider how this affects the **name** parameter. More parameters just multiply their effects.

So what does this mean? Fewer parameters are usually a good thing, which simplifies our methods and makes them easier to understand and test. How do we handle existing methods with too many parameters?

```
1   def start_game(num_players, start_score, number_of_rounds,
        score_to_win, network_game)
2       # confirm the parameters provided are correct
3       # start a new game
4   end
```

The method **start_game** has many parameters. As you scan the method definition, you notice that the shear number of parameters makes the method hard to comprehend. Each parameter has a relationship with another. The parameter **network_game** affects the valid values for **num_players**. A local game might only have a max player count of 4, while a network game could have 64. These parameter interactions can be an enormous mental strain, so grouping them into a single class is a great start to help.

Now see this example:

```
1   class Config
2     attr_accessor :num_players, :start_score, :number_of_
        rounds, :score_to_win, :network_game
3
4     def initialize(num_players, start_score, number_of_
        rounds, score_to_win, network_game)
5       # Confirm the parameters provided are correct
6
7       # Assign instance variables
8       @num_players = num_players
9       @start_score = start_score
10      @number_of_rounds = number_of_rounds
```

```
11      @score_to_win = score_to_win
12      @network_game = network_game
13    end
14  end
15
16  # separate method that starts the game
17  def start_game(game_config)
18   # start a new game
19  end
20
21  # config values
22  player_count = 4
23  score = 0
24  rounds = 2
25  winning_score = 10
26  is_network_game = false
27
28  # create a config
29  game_config = Config.new(player_count, score, rounds,
    winning_score, is_network_game)
30
31  # start the game using the config
32  start_game(game_config)
```

By encapsulating the parameters with a class used in the *start_game*
method definition, the number of parameters decreases from 5 to 1.
In addition, the responsibility of validating the config data now falls to
the **Config** class instead of the **start_game** method. The clarity of the
method definition improved with only a single parameter. The reader
can investigate the Config class if they need more information, but not to
understand the **start_game** method.

With configuration values wrapped in a **Config** class, other methods can use that class without duplicating associated validation and logic. The addition and removal of configuration items doesn't force the method definition to change. Invoking the method stays untouched, but any place that initializes **Config** will still need to change. We can fix this by taking our parameter refactor one step further.

```ruby
1    class Game
2      def initialize(config)
3        @config = config
4      end
5
6      # Formerly the start_game method
7      def start
8        # start a new game using @config
9      end
10   end
11
12   # config values
13   player_count = 4
14   score = 0
15   rounds = 2
16   winning_score = 10
17   is_network_game = false
18
19   # create a config
20   game_config = Config.new(player_count, score, rounds,
     winning_score, is_network_game)
21
22   game = Game.new(game_config)
23   game.start
```

I have moved the **start_game** method to a new class **Game** (renamed **start**). An instance of the **Config** class passed to **Game** initialization eliminates the need for passing to **start**. Every time a new game is started, it reuses the config. Several refactors have reduced the original **start_game** from 5 to 0 parameter. The result is a simple method definition that is easy to understand.

You improve method definitions by limiting the number of parameters. This doesn't mean you need to drop parameters altogether, but just watch how you use them. Although it might be easy to add one more parameter to a method you're changing, it's better to evolve your code to meet your needs. Challenge yourself to consider different approaches to solve a problem and not take shortcuts.

Parameter Order

The order parameters appear in a method definition plays a role how other developers understand that method. Think how you describe a cake recipe to a friend. Your friend expects to receive the baking steps in a specific order. If you deliver the recipe in an order counter to what your friend expects, this will confuse them. Here is an example of steps in the wrong order:

- Bake time

- Icing ingredients

- Mix instructions for the cake batter

Now they have the steps, but your friend would need to reorder them before starting. Parameters carry a similar expectation. Parameter order counter to common expectations will confuse future developers.

Here's an example:

```
1   def login(password, username)
2   # do user login
3   end
```

The method defines **password** before **username**. Most developers would expect them to be reversed. This expectation is so ingrained that many people would call the method in the manner they're used to without looking at the method definition.

Consider the next example:

```
1   login(username, password)
```

We call the **login** method using the expected parameter order of **username** and then **password**. This method usage looks legitimate. Both parameters are strings so the method will execute, but the user can never login. This bug can be hard to spot since the expectation for the method differs from the actual method definition. More complex methods with many parameters add to the confusion.

When you create a method, consider the order of the parameters and how they relate to each other. The most important parameters should be first. Make sure the next parameter makes sense in the order presented. Try calling the method and see if the parameter order makes sense.

Return Values

Ruby doesn't restrict the values you return from a method. A method can return a string as well as a hash. This flexibility is powerful but may cause other problems. Methods encapsulate behavior, hiding details from other parts of the code. Creating a method that returns multiple types of values creates a coupling between the method and the calling code. To use the method, the calling code has to understand how the method works. I now expose the details that were hidden. If I introduce more return types, the calling code will need to be changed. This is not ideal.

```ruby
1   class User
2     attr_accessor :id, :name
3
4     def initialize(id, name)
5       self.id = id
6       self.name = name
7     end
8   end
9
10  def find_by_name(users, name)
11    users.each do |user|
12      if user.name == name
13        return user
14      end
15    end
16
17    return { message: "Unable to find user with name #{name}" }
18  end
19
20  users = []
21  users << User.new(1, "Alice")
22  users << User.new(2, "Joe")
23
24  find_by_name(users, 'Alice')
```

Here we have a method that finds a user by name. The code iterates through the collection of users and returns the user with the matching name. If the method finds no user, it returns a **Hash** with a message. The method has two possible value types: instance of the **User** class or a **Hash**. The calling code will need to check which type of value is returned to avoid issues.

```
1   user = find_by_name(users, "Jane")
2   if user.is_a?(Hash) && !user[:message].nil?
3     puts user[:message]
4   else
5     puts user.id
6   end
```

Changing the return value type creates distrust in a method. The reader won't know if the method returns two types of values or more? Nor will they know if the number of return types will change? We don't want developers asking such questions about our code.

In the next example, we remove the last line that returns a Hash.

```
1   def find_by_name(users, name)
2     users.each do |user|
3       if user.name == name
4         return user
5       end
6     end
7   end
8
9   users = []
10  users << User.new(1, "Alice")
11  users << User.new(2, "Joe")
12
```

```
13   user = find_by_name(users, "Jane")
14
15   if user.nil?
16     puts "No user found"
17   else
18     puts user.id
19   end
```

Since the return value can only be an instance of a **User**, the calling code need not check the return type. The calling code takes the responsibility of crafting a message to display if it finds no user, but that is a reasonable choice.

The original **find_by_name** is frustrating to work with, because you're never sure what type of value will be return. Each developer who uses the method will end up needing to read the method to make sure they haven't missed something. Returning a single value type eliminates the need to do this.

Guard Clause

The data provided to a method may not be valid. If a method expects a string, the calling code might accidentally pass a numeric value. A guard clause at the top of a method creates a safe environment for the rest of the method to work.

```
1   def clear(items)
2     return if items.nil? || !items.is_a?(Array)
3     items.each do |item|
4       # clear the item
5     end
6   end
```

The first line in the method checks that **items** is not nil and is of type Array. The rest of the method is free to use **items** with no need to check it. This can remove much code and prevent ugly nesting. The code is easier to read since the expectations of the **items** parameter are at the top of the method and not hidden throughout.

Length

Most methods have humble beginnings, but they grow larger. Any method should not take on too much responsibility. How do you decide when a method is doing too much? The method length is a good sign. If you create a method with hundreds of lines of Ruby code, we can say with certainty that the method is doing too much. Short, succinct methods often have a single role.

How do we know if a method is too long? This isn't an exact science. Your method is too long, if it has hundreds of lines of code. A method of about 20 lines might be harder to figure whether it's too long. Ruby is a high-level language that can do much in a single line, with less need for boilerplate code to do simple tasks such as creating a network connection to another server. You should be able to carry out most tasks with few lines of code. Methods with more than five lines of code should be investigated further to find if a problem exists.

How to Shorten a Method

What happens when you find a method that is too long? What do you do? One technique is to find any logical grouping of statements that have a common purpose and use them to form new methods. The original method then calls the new methods. After refactoring, the original method no longer needs to know the details of the code we've moved. Any change to the new methods doesn't affect the original method.

```ruby
1   # Too long example
2   def create_user(first_name, last_name)
3     if first_name.nil? || first_name == "
4       raise ArgumentError, 'first_name is required'
5     end
6
7     if last_name.nil? || first_name == "
8       raise ArgumentError, 'first_name is required'
9     end
10
11    User.create(
12      first_name: first_name,
13      last_name: last_name
14    )
15  end
```

In this example, we start with a single method. The method has just seven lines of code, but further examination shows a Single Responsibility Principle violation. The method has two responsibilities: confirm input parameters, and create a user. Validation shouldn't be in the **create_user** method; let's refactor.

```ruby
1   # Shorter example
2   def create_user(first_name, last_name)
3     validate_input(first_name, last_name)
4     User.create(
5       first_name: first_name,
6       last_name: last_name
7     )
8   end
9
10  def validate_input(first_name, last_name)
```

```
11    if first_name.nil? || first_name == "
12      raise ArgumentError, 'first_name is required'
13    end
14
15    if last_name.nil? || last_name == "
16      raise ArgumentError, 'last_name is required'
17    end
18  end
```

In the second example, I move the validation code to a new method called **validate_input**. The new method has one responsibility to confirm parameters used to create a user. The **create_user** method now calls **validate_input** and just creates the user, since validation is the responsibility of another method. As an added benefit, future changes to the validation logic do not need a change to the **create_user** method.

Too Short

A method should be short and concise, but you can make a method too short, where understanding can be challenging. Short methods pack too much information on a single line.

```
1   # Multiple Lines
2   def qualified_users
3     active_users = User.where(active: true)
4     qualified_users = active_users.select(&:qualified?)
5     qualified_users.sort(&:last_login)
6   end
```

The example method **qualified_users** fetches a list of qualified users from the database. I do this using three lines of code. The first line retrieves the active users. The second line selects users marked as qualified. The third line sorts the qualified users by their last login date. Breaking complex operations into smaller digestible pieces makes the method easier to follow.

Now this example has the same steps but is written as a single line of code.

```
1   # Single Line
2   def qualified_users
3     User.where(active: true).select(&:qualified?).sort(&:last_
      login)
4   end
```

We've eliminated the variables **qualified_users** and **active_users** and placed the select and sort statement inline. Reading the single line requires the reader to keep track of everything at once. As the line of code gets longer, the reader must keep more information in their head, and they won't be able to understand it. Keep your lines short.

If you must chain your method calls, break the call chain into multiple lines.

```
1   # Single Line
2   def qualified_users
3     User.where(active: true)
4       .select(&:qualified?)
5       .sort(&:last_login)
6   end
```

Chaining method calls using this syntax is easier to follow since each call is on its on line.

Comments

Much thought goes into writing a line of code. In an ideal world, our code expresses these thoughts concisely. That isn't always the case. Existing code and third-party libraries can introduce hacks and workarounds that are hard to communicate with code alone. After solving a difficult problem,

we don't want to lose the gained knowledge. This is where code comments
are helpful. A comment provides more information and communicates
assumptions for one or more lines of code. When another developer reads
the comment, they won't have to rediscover and solve the problems you
encountered.

Comments sound great, so why not use them everywhere? While
comments are helpful, it's possible to overuse them:

```
1   def change_role(user_id, new_role)
2    # find a user by id
3    user = User.find(user_id)
4
5    # check that current role does not equal the new role
6    if user.role != new_role
7     # assign new role to the user
8     user.role = new_role
9    end
10   # end of method
11  end
```

Every line has a comment. Each comment describes a line of code, but
the code already does this. Consider the first line:

```
1   user = User.find(user_id)
```

The statement is straightforward; it finds a user with an id, and a
comment gives no new information. It's redundant and only doubles
the lines of code the reader has to parse. Do the other comments
communicate something you can't understand from the code alone? The
next example removes all comments:

```
1   def change_role(user_id, new_role)
2    user = User.find(user_id)
3
```

```
4   if user.role != new_role
5     user.role = new_role
6   end
7   end
```

The method is the same minus comments. By removing the comments, the method hasn't suffered in its readability. In fact, the method might even be more readable. If you discover comments in an existing codebase, ask yourself if deleting them removes important information. If you want to add comments, ask yourself if that adds more information not communicated by the code.

Quality Comments

A good comment provides knowledge that's important for the developer attempting to understand the code. Comments don't need exact syntax because Ruby does not interpret them. It's still important to treat comments with respect. Spelling mistakes and misleading information can do more harm than not having a comment. So what is a good comment? See this next example.

```
1    def change_role(user_id, new_role)
2      user = User.find(user_id)
3
4      role_service = RoleService.new(user)
5
6      # Roles cannot be downgraded so the role service will
7      # return false if the new role is 'less' then the
8      # current role
9      return unless role_service.can_assign(new_role)
10
```

```
11    if user.role != new_role
12      user.role = new_role
13    end
14  end
```

It adds a new line:

```
1   return unless role_service.can_assign(new_role)
```

This line of code includes a comment that provides added information. The comment informs the reader of the RoleService limitations, which might be difficult to communicate in code alone. If we removed the comment, the reader loses valuable information. So it's a good comment.

Stale Comments

Comments can cause problems if someone does not keep them up to date. Changing a line of code can make a comment no longer valid. Deleting code without removing associated comments will cause problems.

```
1   def fullname(first_name, last_name)
2     # Confirm last_name is not blank or nil
3     "#{first_name} #{last_name}".strip
4   end
```

The method **fullname** takes two values and concatenates them to create a string that is a full name. The comment in the method accompanied a line of code that validated the **last_name** parameter. Someone removed the validation code, but not the comment. The first thing a developer reads is an incorrect comment. In a larger method, this can add mental overhead.

Don't allow comments to go stale. If you refactor code, make sure you remove or update any comments you find.

Comments and Refactoring

Comments can group related statements. For longer methods, this kind of comment offers a guide. Each comment explains what the group of statements do. While helpful, it's a clear sign that the method needs refactoring, as shown here.

```ruby
1   def accounts_from_file(file_path)
2     # read lines from file
3     file = File.new(file_path)
4     lines = file.readlines
5
6     # Create an account for each line
7     accounts = lines.collect do |line|
8       # Parse name and email
9       account_info = line.parse(',')
10      name = account_info[0]
11      email = account_info[1]
12
13      # Create an account using the parsed data
14      Account.create(name: name, email: email)
15    end
16  end
```

Each comment explains an operation. The first group of statements reads a file. Then the method creates an account for each line in the file. Inside the collect block, we parse a single line and an account created using the attributes. Each comment is an opportunity to refactor. Let's use the comments to create new methods.

```ruby
1   def accounts_from_file(file_path)
2     lines = read_file(file_path)
3     create_accounts(lines)
4   end
```

```
 5
 6  def read_file(file_path)
 7    file = File.new(file_path)
 8    file.readlines
 9  end
10
11  def create_accounts(lines)
12    accounts = lines.collect do |line|
13      account_params = account_params_from_line(line)
14      Account.create(account_params)
15    end
16  end
17
18  def account_params_from_line(line)
19    account_info = line.parse(',')
20    { name: account_info[0], email: account_info[1] }
21  end
```

We've turned each comment into a method. Instead of relying on comments to tell a story, we use the code. The original method had too many responsibilities. It reads the file, parsed each line, and created accounts using the data. Each responsibility has no relation to another besides being used for account creation. The new example divides responsibilities into multiple methods. Each method handles one task and is independent of one another. The independence provides room for code reuse beyond the original intent.

Limit Nesting

Nested statements in a method are often a sign of complexity. You can spot them because too many nested statements make the method resemble a wave, or a greater-than symbol (>).

```
1    MAX_PROMO_RATE = 5
2
3    def send_promo_email(user)
4      if user.email.present?
5        if user.promos_sent < MAX_PROMO_RATE
6          UserMailer.promo_email(user).deliver
7        end
8      end
9    end
```

This code sends a promo email to the specified user. The method has two "if" statements, one nested inside the other. The first "if" statement checks whether the user has an email. The second "if" statement checks if we exceeded the promo threshold. If all boolean tests are true, we send a promo email. There are only two levels of nesting, but even this level of nesting makes the method hard to understand. This code needs refactoring:

```
1    MAX_PROMO_RATE = 5
2
3    def send_promo_email(user)
4      if can_send?(user)
5        UserMailer.promo_email(user).deliver
6      end
7    end
8
9    def can_send?(user)
10     user.email.present? && user.promos_sent < MAX_PROMO_RATE
11   end
```

I have abstracted the boolean tests to a new method "**can_send?**". It encapsulates the boolean logic in one method. This eliminates the nesting and makes the method easier to understand. If you read the "**send_promo_email**" method, you don't have to understand how "**can_send?**" works to comprehend what the method does. If we need to add a condition, **send_promo_email** won't need to be changed.

CHAPTER 4

Using Boolean Logic

Software consists mostly of testing data and determining whether certain conditions are true or false. Every program makes thousands of these decisions. Since boolean logic is so vital to an application, it's important to take care when programming them. A single boolean statement is easy to understand, but complex logic with two or more boolean statements can be hard to understand, making it hard to maintain and the source of bugs. Even small improvements to boolean logic can help prevent misunderstandings. In this chapter, we will discuss different techniques you can use. Each method has pros and cons. Check each option before choosing the one correct for a situation.

Using a Variable

As we learned in earlier chapters, we use variables to store data. They describe data, so other developers know what it is. Boolean values, like numbers and strings, gain context when stored in a variable. A boolean variable helps future readers understand what the boolean represents. This is useful for complex logic needed to determine if something is true or false. Storing the result of a boolean statement in a variable removes the need for other developers to parse the complex logic. The variable name provides the information they need. Look at this example.

© Carleton DiLeo 2019
C. DiLeo, *Clean Ruby*, https://doi.org/10.1007/978-1-4842-5546-9_4

```ruby
1   class Player
2     attr_accessor :time_until_spawn, :health
3   end
4
5   # Boolean logic directly in an IF statement
6   def respawn(player)
7     if player.time_until_spawn <= 0 && player.health == 0
8       respawn_at_base
9     end
10  end
11
12  def respawn_at_base
13    puts 'Player respawned at base'
14  end
15
16  player = Player.new
17  player.time_until_spawn = 0
18  player.health = 0
19
20  respawn(player)
```

The example has the method **respawn**. It has two boolean statements that check if the player's time until spawn is less than or equal to 0 and if the player's health is equal to 0. If both statements are true, we respawn the player at their base. The logic isn't difficult, but might not be clear to the reader. This isn't ideal since we want the reader to comprehend our code with minimal effort. Let's improve the example by introducing a variable.

```ruby
1   class Player
2     attr_accessor :time_until_spawn, :health
3   end
4
```

```ruby
5    # Boolean logic stored in a variable
6    def respawn(player)
7      ready_to_spawn = player.time_until_spawn <= 0 &&
8        player.health == 0
9      respawn_at_base if ready_to_spawn
10   end
11
12   def respawn_at_base
13     puts 'Player respawned at base'
14   end
15
16   player = Player.new
17   player.time_until_spawn = 0
18   player.health = 0
19
20   respawn(player)
```

The second example takes the results of the boolean statement and stores it in the variable **ready_to_respawn**. The name of the variable tells the reader why the boolean statement exists. While the reader can parse the boolean statement in its entirety, it's not required. The variable name provides enough detail. The purpose of the boolean statement is clear: it checks if the player is "ready to spawn."

Using a variable provides useful hints but can have unintended side effects. The next example determines if we allow a user to edit articles.

```ruby
1    class User
2      attr_accessor :type, :enabled
3
4      def initialize(type, enabled)
5        @type = type
6        @enabled = enabled
7      end
```

```
8
9    def editor?
10     type == :editor
11   end
12
13   def disabled?
14     !enabled
15   end
16 end
17
18 user = User.new(:editor, true)
19
20 if !user.nil? && user.editor? && !user.disabled?
21   puts 'The user is allowed to edit articles'
22 end
```

The first boolean statement ensures that the user object is not **nil** before performing more checks. If the user is **nil**, then we will evaluate none of the following tests. It avoids the possibility of an error due if the user is **nil**. We call this concept "short-circuiting." The next example splits the boolean logic and stores the result into two variables.

```
1  def enable_editing
2    user_exists = !user.nil?
3    can_edit = user.editor? && !user.disabled?
4
5    if user_exists && can_edit
6      # code to enable editing
7    end
8  end
```

The new code reads nicely but will cause an error if the "user" object is **nil**. Even if the user is **nil**, the second line will still execute. It's possible to fix this by adding a guard statement.

```
1   def enable_editing
2     user_exists = !user.nil?
3     return if user_exists
4
5     can_edit = user.editor? && !user.disabled?
6
7     if user_exists && can_edit
8       # code to enable editing
9     end
10  end
```

Be careful if you use this approach when refactoring boolean logic. If used correctly, it can be the first step to making your logic more readable.

Using a Method

The last section used a variable to store a boolean value, but this doesn't always work. Some code requires you to do boolean checks in order. Using a variable isn't the only way to refactor boolean logic. Methods offer a great way to abstract the details of our code.

```
1   class Order
2     attr_accessor :items, :purchase_date
3
4     def initialize(items, purchase_date)
5       @items = items
6       @purchase_date = purchase_date
7     end
8   end
```

```
 9
10   class Item
11    attr_accessor :delivered
12
13    def initialize(delivered)
14     @delivered = delivered
15    end
16
17    def delivered?
18     delivered
19    end
20   end
21
22   def send_order_followup_email(order)
23    all_items_delivered = true
24    order.items.each do |item|
25     if !item.delivered?
26      all_items_delivered = false
27      break
28     end
29    end
30
31    order_delivered = all_items_delivered && order.purchase_
     date < Time.now
32
33    if order_delivered
34     # Send follow up email
35     puts "Sent follow up email"
36    else
37     puts "Not all items delivered"
```

```
38    end
39  end
40
41  # Here we run the code
42  items = [Item.new(false), Item.new(true)]
43  order = Order.new(items, Time.now)
44
45  send_order_followup_email(order)
```

In this example, the method **send_order_followup_email** uses a variable to store whether or not an order was delivered. Using a variable helps make the code more readable, but it is better to move the boolean logic to a separate method.

```
1   class Order
2     attr_accessor :items, :purchase_date
3
4     def initialize(items, purchase_date)
5       @items = items
6       @purchase_date = purchase_date
7     end
8   end
9
10  class Item
11    attr_accessor :delivered
12
13    def initialize(delivered)
14      @delivered = delivered
15    end
16
17    def delivered?
```

```
18    delivered
19   end
20  end
21
22  def send_order_followup_email(order)
23   if order_delivered?(order)
24    # Send follow up email
25    puts "Sent follow up email"
26   else
27    puts "Not all items delivered"
28   end
29  end
30
31  def order_delivered?(order)
32   all_items_delivered = true
33
34   order.items.each do |item|
35    if !item.delivered?
36     all_items_delivered = false
37     break
38    end
39   end
40
41   all_items_delivered && order.purchase_date < Time.now
42  end
43
44  # Here we run the code
45  items = [Item.new(false), Item.new(true)]
46  order = Order.new(items, Time.now)
47
48  send_order_followup_email(order)
```

The new method **order_delivered?** determines if we delivered an order. The **send_order_follow_up_email** method calls **order_delivered?**. The name of the new method informs the reader what the result of the boolean logic is. Also, we can change the logic that determines if we delivered an order with no need to touch **send_order_follow_up_email**. We can reuse the code, if needed. An additional method allows for easier and better unit testing.

Unless

The **unless** statement is the inverse of an **If** statement. An **if** statement tests whether a statement is true, where **unless** tests if a statement is false. When used correctly, it can make your code more readable, but using **unless** can be difficult.

```
1   if !user_authenticated?
2     # do something
3   end
```

The **if** statement checks whether a user is *not* authenticated. Using **unless** eliminates the need to use an exclamation point.

```
1   unless user_authenticated?
2     # Do something
3   end
```

At first glance, this seems easier to read. For some readers, it can be difficult to understand the code inside the **unless** block only executes if the statement to the right of the **unless** is false. If the **unless** statement has multiple boolean statements, the reader might need to use a pen and paper to figure out what's happening. We should avoid any code that requires this level of analysis. We want other developers to understand our code with little thought. I recommend not using **unless**, if possible.

Ternary Operator

Less code is better. More code means more to read and more chances for mistakes. Turning lines of code into a single statement can create tight, readable code.

```
1  if a > b
2    result = "A is greater"
3  else
4    result = "B is greater"
5  end
```

This example is easy to read, but verbose. Shortening it would be less code. **Ternary operators** change such boolean statements into a single line. Instead of using an **If** statement, we place the boolean logic on a single line with a variable assignment. The statement before "?" is the boolean check; the two strings to its right are values assigned to variable "result" depending on whether the statement is true. We will assign the first string if the boolean statement equals true; we will assign the second value if false.

```
1  result = a > b ? "A is greater": "B is greater"
```

Using the ternary operator condenses the code into a single line of code. We also removed duplication and made the variable assignment clearer.

While ternary operators can improve your code, they also create hard-to-read code, since complicated boolean statements will be confusing.

```
1  result = logged_in? && admin? ? "Admin logged In": "Admin
   is not logged In"
```

This example is hard to read. There are multiple conditions that determine if an admin is logged in. This is an example where using the ternary operate places too much information on a single line:

```
1    if logged_in? && admin?
2      result = "Admin logged In"
3    else
4      result = "Admin is not logged In"
5    end
```

Using an **if** statement is more verbose but will be easier to read. Like most tools in Ruby, be cautious and use good judgment when using the ternary operator. Use ternary operators when the boolean statement is short. Opt for the longer **if** syntax, when the boolean statement is long.

Double Negative

Our brains are good at understanding boolean statements that are true or false. Problems arise when the boolean logic has double negatives, with statements where the value must be **not not** false. Even the sentence describing a double negative is hard to understand. Let's use an example to make it clearer.

```
1    class Book
2      attr_accessor :name
3
4      def initialize(name)
5        self.name = name
6      end
7    end
8
9    class Library
10     attr_accessor :books
11
```

```
12    def initialize(books)
13      self.books = books
15    end
16
17    def is_not_found(book)
18      found = self.books.include?(book)
19      !found
20    end
21  end
22
23  book1 = Book.new('Ready Player One')
24  book2 = Book.new('Armada')
25
26  books = [book1, book2]
27  library = Library.new(books)
28
29  if !library.is_not_found(book2)
30    puts "#{book2.name} is in the library"
31  end
```

This example has two classes: **Book** and **Library**. We create two books
and add them to the library. We check if the library does **not not** contain
book2 and display a message only if the statement is true. The **if** statement
is using a double negative, turning what should be a simple statement
into one hard to understand. Coding boolean logic this way is like asking
someone if they "wouldn't not" like you to pass the salt. Untangling the
logic in the example is difficult. The solution is simple:

```
1  class Book
2    attr_accessor :name
3
4    def initialize(name)
5      self.name = name
```

```
 6    end
 7  end
 8
 9
10  class Library
11    attr_accessor :books
12
13    def initialize(books)
14      self.books = books
15    end
16
17    def is_found(book) # <= We change the method
18      self.books.include?(book)
19    end
20  end
21
22  book1 = Book.new('Ready Player One')
23  book2 = Book.new('Armada')
24
25  books = [book1, book2]
26  library = Library.new(books)
27
28  if library.is_found(book2) # <= This is much clearer
29    puts "#{book2.name} is in the library"
30  end
```

We've made two changes. The first is changing **is_not_found** to
is_found inside the **Library** class. Then we updated the **if** statement to
use the new method. The only thing we've done is reversing the boolean
statement. Instead of using a double negative, we check if we find the
book. The result is a boolean statement that is much easier to follow.

Truthy and Falsy

Boolean values aren't the only values that are **true** and **false**. In Ruby, all data has an associated **true** or **false** value. It considers values like **nil** falsy, while it deems others truthy. What are "truthy" and "falsy"? When we say a value is truthy, we are saying Ruby considers it true in a boolean statement even though not explicitly true. For example, it considers the number 4 as **true**, so it is truthy, while it treats **nil** as **false**, or falsy.

```
1   name = "Carleton"
2   if name
3     puts "My first name is #{name}"
4   end
```

In this example, we check if **name** is true and display "My first name is Carleton", if it is. Since **name** is a string with characters, Ruby evaluates it as true.

```
1   last_name = nil
2   if last_name
3     puts "My last name is #{last_name}"
4   end
```

This example checks if **last_name** is true. Since **last_name** is **nil**, Ruby considers it as **false**. Knowing which values are truthy and falsy can help you write code that's shorter and more expressive. The following is a list of truthy and falsy values for Ruby.

Truthy Values

- 0
- 20
- " "

- "Value"

- true

- TRUE

- [3,4,5]

- { first: 'one' }

Falsy Values

- nil

- false

- FALSE

& vs. &&

Sometimes you will see boolean statements that use a single "&" instead of two. At first glance, there doesn't seem to be a difference between the two operators. Deeper examination uncovers a small, but significant, difference that can be useful and a source of bugs. Knowing the difference will help you make the right choice when coding a boolean statement. This example uses a single "&."

```
1   class User
2     attr_accessor :type
3
4     def initialize(type)
5       @type = type
6     end
7   end
8
```

```
 9   first_user = User.new(:regular)
10   second_user = nil
11
12   if first_user.type == :admin & second_user.type == :admin
13     puts 'Both users are an admin'
14   else
15     puts 'Both users are not admin'
16   end
```

Here we have a **User** with an attribute that signifies its type, such as an admin. Next, we create an instance of **User** and set it as type **:regular**. We also create a **second_user** as **nil**. The **if** statement checks if **first_user** and **second_user** are of type admin. Since **second_user** is **nil**, the result of the code should be "Both users are not admin" being printed to the screen. Running the code uncovers an error.

```
1   SyntaxError: (irb):11: syntax error, unexpected ==
2   first_user.type == :admin & second_user.type == :admin
```

The single "&" evaluates both statements regardless of the outcome of the first statement. This can be useful, but it creates a bug here.

```
 1   class User
 2     attr_accessor :type
 3
 4     def initialize(type)
 5       @type = type
 6     end
 7   end
 8
 9   first_user = User.new(:regular)
10   second_user = nil
11
```

```
12  if first_user.type == :admin && second_user.type == :admin
13    puts 'Both users are an admin'
14  else
15    puts 'Both users are not admin'
16  end
```

We've changed the statement from a single "&" to a double "&&". Since the first statement `first_user.type == :admin` is false, the double && won't evaluate the second statement because the second statement won't make the combined result true.

As a general rule, use double "&&" when you want to prevent evaluating the second boolean statement, if the first statement is false. If you want both statements evaluated regardless of whether the first statement is true, use a single "&".

CHAPTER 5

Classes

In this chapter, we cover several techniques you can use to make high-quality classes.

Initialize Method

When instantiating a class in Ruby, the **new** class method calls the **initialize** instance method. Any parameters passed to the **new** method will be passed to the initialize method. The **initialize** method is a setup method for a class. It's called before any other method defined in the class. If we have steps to perform before using the class, we place them in the initialize method. Let's look at techniques we can use to improve our **initialize** methods.

Keep It Simple

The **initialize** method should be simple, which means limiting operations to things such as assignments. Move complex operations outside of the initialize method and call after class creation. Keeping the **initialize** method simple avoids surprises. Let's look at an example:

```
1   class BankAccount
2     def initialize(number)
3       @number = number
4       external_account = ExternalBankAccount.new
```

```
5      external_account.load_balances(@number)
6      external_account.sync_transactions
7    end
8  end
9
10   bank_account = BankAccount.new("1234")
```

In this example, there is a **BankAccount** class with an **initialize** method which performs several tasks. First, we assign the value of the parameter **number** to the instance variable **number**. Next, we load external account bank data using the **ExternalBankAccount** class, and we sync transactions from the bank account. We don't know the exact details of the **External-BankAccount** class, but it's implied that it will fetch data from an external data source.

External data calls are slow and error-prone. These operations are not the responsibility of the **initialize** method. It will catch other developers offguard when initializing **BankAccount**, and we never want to surprise people with our code.

Let's move the **BankAccount** code to a separate method and call it after we instantiate the class.

```
1  class BankAccount
2    def initialize(number)
3      @number = number
4    end
5
6    def load_bank_account
7      external_account = ExternalBankAccount.new
8      external_account.load_balances(@number)
9      external_account.sync_transactions
10   end
11 end
```

```
12
13   bank_account = BankAccount.new("1234")
14   bank_account.load_external_accounts
```

We created a new method called **load_bank_account** and moved .
the code that loads the bank account. We call the new method after
instantiating our class. Even though we introduced another step, the
intention is much clearer. Creating an instance of the **BankAccount** class
only stores data from parameters. An added method performs more
complex operations. This change makes the class more flexible. We can
call **load_external_accounts** right after creating our class, or later if
needed. Besides flexibility, it will not surprise other developers.

Avoiding Errors

We touched upon this in the last section. It's best to avoid error-prone
code in the **initialize** method. An initialize method that throws an
exception because of a database connection failure is not an expected
outcome. Since we usually don't wrap object creation in **begin/rescue**, the
exception will go unhandled and cause unexpected problems.

While we should avoid creating initialize methods that throw errors,
exceptions are acceptable if the resulting object will be malformed and
unusable. For example, you might raise an ArgumentError when the
initialize method receives invalid data. This avoids the need for **nil** value
checks or type checking every time we use the value. It removes duplicate
code and allows the calling code to know that the object is invalid sooner.
Look at this example.

```
1   class BankAccount
2     def initialize(number)
3       raise ArgumentError, 'number cannot be nil' if number.nil?
```

```
4     @number = number
5   end
6 end
```

. Here we check if the number provided is not **nil**. If the number is **nil**, we raise an error because a **nil** value causes problems. The calling code should rescue the ArgumentError and give a new value. Sometimes we might want object creation to fail, but we should do so only because continuing to use the object causes further errors.

Too Many Parameters

Any method using too many parameters is more complex and difficult to change. We call the **initialize** method every time we create an object, and that happens often in an application. This means any changes to the initialize method will have a ripple effect throughout the code. Let's look at an example:

```
1 class Property
2   def initialize(street, street2, city, state, zipcode)
3     @street = street
4     @street2 = street2
5     @city = city
6     @state = state
7     @zipcode = zipcode
8   end
9 end
```

Here we have the class **Property**. The initialize method for this class accepts many parameters. This isn't ideal for many reasons. Having this many parameters makes initializing a class hard to understand. Also, remembering the order in which we need to provide the parameters can be tough. Let's improve the code by moving parameters to a new class. We will then change the initialize method to accept the class instead of a bunch of parameters. This provides more context to the data and makes the code cleaner.

```
1   class Address
2     def initialize(street, street2, city, state, zipcode)
3       @street = street
4       @street2 = street2
5       @city = city
6       @state = state
7       @zipcode = zipcode
8     end
9   end
10
11  class Property
12    def initialize(address)
13      @address = address
14    end
15  end
```

We've moved all the parameters to a new class called **Address**. Now the **Property** class requires only a single parameter. As an added advantage, we hide the details of the address from the **Property** class, which helps reduces its responsibilities. Even though we only moved the parameters from one class to another, we can now reuse the **Address** class in other parts of the code. We can test this new class and add functionality without affecting the **Property** class.

Class Methods vs. Instance Methods

Not all methods should be instance methods. When defining a method, you have two options, an instance method and a class method. A class method exists within the context of a class, but cannot interact with a class's data and is not callable by an instance of the class. These methods perform actions related to the class itself, not an instance of the class.

```
1    class Car
2      def initialize(year, make, model)
3        @year = year
4        @make = make
5        @model = model
6      end
7    end
8
9    def create_car(make, model)
10     current_year = Time.now.year
11     Car.new(current_year, make, model)
12   end
13
14   car = create_car('Nissan', 'Altima')
```

In this example, the **Car** class has the attributes; make, model, and year. Next, the method **create_car** creates an instance of **Car** for the current year using the provided make and model. The method is defined outside of the **Car** class even though executing it only makes sense in a **Car** context. If the method is placed in a different file, it will be hard to find. Converting the method into a class method will fix that.

```
1    class Car
2      def initialize(year, make, model)
3        @year = year
```

```
4      @make = make
5      @model = model
6    end
7
8    def self.create
9        current_year = Time.now.year
10        new(current_year, make, model)
11    end
12  end
13
14  car = Car.create('Nissan', 'Altima')
```

The **create_car** method is moved into the **Car** class and renamed **create**. Since the method is inside the **Car** class, other developers will see it and most likely use it in their code. This means it's less likely they will duplicate the code present in another method.

Instance variables

Instance variables have class-level scope. Instead of having scope limited to a single method, they stay in memory for the life of an object. This means an instance variable is accessible from any method in a class. We could make all variables in a class instance variables, but this will cause problems. Since instance variables are accessible throughout a class, we wouldn't be able to prevent methods from stepping over each other. Calling one method might change a variable used in another. Choosing when to use instance variables is an important part of defining a class, and will help limit the need to pass around data between methods.

How do we decide when to use an instance variable? Let's look at the following example to find out.

```ruby
 1   require 'date'
 2
 3   class WelcomeMailer
 4    def self.send(email)
 5     puts "Sending welcome email to #{email}..."
 6    end
 7   end
 8
 9   class User
10    attr_accessor :email, :subscription_expired_at
11    def initialize(email)
12     @email = email
13     @subscription_expired_at = DateTime.now
14    end
15
16    def login
17     puts "Logging #{@email} in..."
18    end
19   end
20
21   class UserSetup
22    def start_trial(user)
23     user.subscription_expired_at = DateTime.now + 30
24    end
25
26    def send_welcome_email(user)
27     WelcomeMailer.send(user.email)
28    end
29
30    def login(user)
31     user.login
32    end
```

```
33   end
34
35   user = User.new('test@tester.com')
36   user_setup = UserSetup.new
37   user_setup.start_trial(user)
38   user_setup.send_welcome_email(user)
39   user_setup.login(user)
```

The **UserSetup** class has three methods that take a single parameter, user. Since these methods require a user, we can say the entire **UserSetup** class depends on user. We can remove the need to pass an instance of user over and over by introducing an instance variable to the class.

```
1    require 'date'
2
3    class WelcomeMailer
4      def self.send(email)
5        puts "Sending welcome email to #{email}..."
6      end
7    end
8
9    class User
10     attr_accessor :email, :subscription_expired_at
11
12     def initialize(email)
13       @email = email
14       @subscription_expired_at = DateTime.now
15     end
16
17     def login
18       puts "Logging #{@email} in..."
19     end
20   end
```

```
21
22    class UserSetup
23      def initialize(user)
24        @user = user
25      end
26
27      def start_trial
28        @user.subscription_expired_at = DateTime.now + 30
29      end
30
31      def send_welcome_email
32        WelcomeMailer.send(@user.email)
33      end
34
35      def login
36        @user.login
37      end
38    end
39
40    user = User.new('test@tester.com')
41    user_setup = UserSetup.new(user)
42    user_setup.start_trial
43    user_setup.send_welcome_email
44    user_setup.login
```

The initialize method now accepts an instance of user and stores it in an instance variable. We removed the **user** parameter from the other three methods. Each method uses the instance variable instead of having it passed as a parameter. The calling code passes an instance of a user to **UserSetup**.

This ends up being much cleaner since we pass the user instance once, not three times.

Private Methods

A class can have many methods, but not all methods should be available from outside code. Those methods are applicable only to methods inside the class. Making every method public can confuse other developers. When defining a class, it's best to offer a small set of public operations while leaving other details hidden. This is one of the main benefits of OOP. Hiding the inner workings of a class prevents tight coupling between classes, and your code will be more flexible. Making non-essential methods private prevents overloading the reader with too many choices. It's our job to consider the class we are building. Picking the correct accessibility for a method will yield dividends in the long run. Look at this example.

```
1   class BankAccount
2     def initialize(starting_balance)
3       @balance = starting_balance
4     end
5
6     def display_balance
7         format_for_display
8     end
9
10    def format_for_display
11        "Account Balance: #{@balance}"
12    end
13  end
```

Here the **BankAccount** class has two methods: **display_balance** and **format_for_display**. The method **display_balance** uses the method **format_for_display** to format the balance for display. In this example, **format_for_display** only applies within the **BankAcount** class. We don't want another developer using **format_for_display**, instead of **display_balance**. To prevent this, we place the keyword **private** before the **format_for_display** method.

```ruby
1    class BankAccount
2      def initialize(starting_balance)
3        @balance = starting_balance
4      end
5
6      def display_balance
7          format_for_display
8      end
9
10     private
11     def format_for_display
12         "Account Balance: #{@balance}"
13     end
14   end
```

If another developer attempts to use **format_for_display** outside the class, they will receive an error. It is now very clear, instead of relying on others to guess our intentions. Since **format_for_display** is private, we don't want it used outside the class. As a bonus, we can change **format_for_display** as much as we want, and be confident our change only affects the code inside of **BankAccount**. This will make refactoring much easier.

Method Order

Developers read code from top to bottom and left to right. If we place methods in a random order, other developers will jump around the class definition, making it hard to follow. Imagine you were reading a book with a random page order. While it's possible to navigate the book since it numbers the pages, you need to page back and forth to do so. After a while, the mental drain from reading will become too much, and you will become lost. Look at this example.

```
1   class AudioPlayer
2     def play_song(song_path)
3       song = load_song(song_path)
4       determine_output_device
5       start(song)
6     end
7
8     private
9       def determine_output_device
10        # Figure out which audio output device to use
11      end
12
13    def start(song)
14      # Start playing the song
15    end
16
17    def load_song(path)
18      # Load the song from the specified path
19    end
20  end
```

Here the class **AudioPlayer** has a single public method, **play_song**, along with three private methods. **play_song** calls **load_song** first, and is defined at the bottom of the class. Next, we call **determine_output_device**, which is defined at the top of the class. Finally, we call **start**, which is defined in the middle of the class. Reading through the class requires you to skip around, which makes it hard to keep focus. If our class were longer (not recommended, but happens in legacy code), it's much easier for the reader to become lost. Let's reorder the methods.

```
1    class AudioPlayer
2      def play_song(song_path)
3          song = load_song(song_path)
4          determine_output_device
5          start(song)
6      end
7
8      private
9      def load_song(path)
10         # Load the song from the specified path
11     end
12
13     def determine_output_device
14         # Figure out which audio output device to use
15     end
16
17     def start(song)
18         # Start playing the song
19     end
20   end
```

We've reordered the private methods to their call order by **play_song**. When the reader looks at **play_song**, each method is below the next making it easier to follow, without the need to jump around the class definition.

Consider the order of your methods. Don't place them randomly throughout the class. Your fellow developers will thank you.

Moving Methods to a Module

A class is a great way to group related methods, but sometimes a class makes little sense. Mathematical operations are a good example. Math isn't a physical object you can hold, but collects formulas used to manipulate numbers. A "Math" class makes little sense, because creating an instance of math doesn't. We still want the ability to reuse these operations throughout our code. Moving them to a module is a great alternative. Let's look at an example:

```ruby
 1  class BankAccount
 2    def initialize(balance, interest_rate)
 3      @balance = balance
 4      @interest = interest_rate
 5    end
 6
 7    def add_to_balance(amount)
 8      @balance = add(@balance, amount)
 9    end
10
11    def calculate_interest
12      multiply(@balance, @interest_rate)
13    end
14
15    private
16    def add(a, b)
17      a + b
18    end
19
20    def multiply(a, b)
21      a * b
22    end
23  end
```

In this example, **BankAccount** has two public and two private methods. The public methods use the private methods to perform mathematical operations. The private methods, **add** and **multiply,** are math operations that don't belong in the **BankAccount** class. Let's move them to a module and use the **include** operator to add them in to **BankAccount**.

```
1    module Math
2      def add(a, b)
3        a + b
4      end
5
6      def multiply(a, b)
7        a * b
8      end
9    end
10
11   class BankAccount
12     include Math
13
14     def initialize(balance, interest_rate)
15       @balance = balance
16       @interest = interest_rate
17     end
18
19     def add_to_balance(amount)
20       @balance = add(@balance, amount)
21     end
22
23     def calculate_interest
24       multiply(@balance, @interest_rate)
25     end
26   end
```

We created a **Math** module and moved the **add** and **multiply** methods there. We can't create an instance of **Math**, but we can include it in the **BankAccount** class. The two methods are now available for the **BankAccount** class. As a result, the **BankAccount** class is shorter and easier to read. Any classes that need these operations can include them as well.

Limiting Inheritance

Creating parent classes to share data and behavior is a great way to remove code duplication. While inheritance can create clean, beautiful code, it's possible to abuse it and wreak havoc on our code. Since we widely use classes, correcting these problems after the fact can be difficult. Three levels of inheritance should be enough most of the time. Once you go beyond this number, you will have several issues.

First, locating code you need will become cumbersome. Each level of inheritance can contain much data or behavior. Since they are so many levels, knowing which class has the code you are looking for might be unclear.

Second, too many levels of inheritance will create many classes. Working with a codebase with hundreds of class files is difficult. We can try to organize these classes using folders and namespaces, but other developers will spend time getting accustomed to the code before they can become efficient.

If you create too many levels of inheritance, try a different technique. Create a separate class that has the common code, instead of creating a parent class.

```
1  class Accountant
2    def file_taxes
3    end
4  end
5
```

```
 6   class SuperMarket
 7     def initialize(accountant)
 8       @accountant = accountant
 9     end
10   end
11
12   class ToyStore
13     def initialize(accountant)
14       @accountant = accountant
15     end
16   end
17
18   accountant = Accountant.new
19   toy_store = ToyStore.new(accountant)
20   super_market = SuperMarket.new(accountant)
```

This example has two classes: **SuperMarket** and **ToyStore**. Both classes represent businesses, and all businesses need to file taxes. We could have created a Business class that held the common method **file_ taxes**; instead, we created the class **Accountant**, which will file the taxes for each business. This concept is called "composition over inheritance." Instead of thinking what a class "is" (inheritance), we think what a class "has" (composition). In our example, the **SuperMarket** and **ToyStore** classes "have" an accountant.

Composition isn't better than using inheritance. Like all the tools available to you, each has its place. Evaluate each situation to determine which one you should use. It will be obvious once you define your class if you chose wisely.

CHAPTER 6

Refactoring

Every new application starts with the purest intentions. A new codebase means an opportunity to create simple, clean code and avoid past mistakes. Even with our best efforts, deadlines and platform constraints will impede these goals and give way to suboptimal solutions and hacks. It's not anyone's fault, it's just something developers do.

As a program gets older, it's inevitable that it will incur "technical debt," which is code we will need to rewrite due to poor design choices and shortcuts used to finish quickly. It's fragile and breaks easily. Technical debt is in the dark corners of an application that no one touches for fear of breaking the application. However, there's a limit, and eventually we need to "pay off" this debt in the form of refactoring, or, in extreme cases, rewriting the entire application.

Since we never want to build up too much debt, we need to be proactive. Every code change to an application is an opportunity to refactor. Refactoring doesn't have to change a large amount of code. It can be small changes that add up to much bigger changes later. If we consistently make changes to improve our code, then the code is always getting better instead of gradually worse.

This chapter covers how to approach refactoring, including various techniques you can use to get started.

© Carleton DiLeo 2019
C. DiLeo, *Clean Ruby*, https://doi.org/10.1007/978-1-4842-5546-9_6

No Change Too Small

One of the most important mindsets to have when approaching refactoring is no change that improves your code is too small. If you get in the habit of making small changes, it will become part of your routine. You will become comfortable refactoring and start making bigger changes. This mindset is contagious. Once you start, it will inspire other developers to follow your example. It begins with a small positive change.

Let's improve some code.

```
1   class Address
2     attr_accessor :street, :zip
3
4     def initialize(street, zip)
5       @street = street
6       @zip = zip
7     end
8   end
9
10  a1 = Address.new("123 Street", 12345)
11  a2 = Address.new("321 Street", nil)
12
13  def prep(a_list)
14    # remove addresses with no zip
15    a_list.reject! { |a| a.zip.nil? }
16
17    # sort addresses by zip
18    a_list.sort_by { |a| a.zip }
19  end
20
21  s_list = prep([a1, a2])
```

In this example, we have a method that prepares a list of addresses by filtering and sorting them. There are several issues with the code, but we will start by making small improvements. Eventually, we will refactor the entire example.

```ruby
1   class Address
2     attr_accessor :street, :zip
3
4     def initialize(street, zip)
5       @street = street
6       @zip = zip
7     end
8   end
9
10  address1 = Address.new("123 Street", 12345)
11  address2 = Address.new("321 Street", nil)
12
13  def prep(addresses)
14    # remove addresses with no zip
15    addresses.reject! { |address| address.zip.nil? }
16
17    # sort addresses by zip
18    addresses.sort_by { |address| address.zip }
19  end
20
21  addresses = prep([address1, address2])
```

The first change is renaming variables. Many of the original variable names were nondescriptive, providing little information of their purpose. We changed variables **a1** and **a2** to **address1** and **address2**, and parameter **a_list** was changed to **addresses**. The block parameter for reject and sort_by, **a**, was changed to **address**. Finally, we renamed the variable that stores the result of **prep** from **s_list** to **addresses**.

Each name change spelled out the name instead of using abbreviations. Abbreviating a variable name makes it shorter but often removes useful information. Most Ruby applications don't have program size requirements, so using full-length names only benefits the codebase.

On another note, we could have renamed **s_list** to **sorted_addresses**, but that doesn't give any useful information to the reader. Knowing the list is sorted won't change how they use the list later in the code. The result of prep is a collection of addresses. Keeping our variable names simple is ideal.

Next, we will change the name of the **prep** method.

```ruby
1   class Address
2     attr_accessor :street, :zip
3
4     def initialize(street, zip)
5       @street = street
6       @zip = zip
7     end
8   end
9
10  address1 = Address.new("123 Street", 12345)
11  address2 = Address.new("321 Street", nil)
12
13  def prepare_addresses(addresses)
14    # remove addresses with no zip
15    addresses.reject! { |address| address.zip.nil? }
16
17    # sort addresses by zip
18    addresses.sort_by { |address| a.zip }
19  end
20
21  addresses = prepare_addresses([address1, address2])
```

The original method name, **prep**, was an abbreviation of prepare. As mentioned earlier, abbreviations save keystrokes but need brain cycles to understand. Changing **prep** to **prepare** isn't much more typing but prevents adding ambiguity. We appended "_addresses" to the end of the method name for added clarity, and now you know what the method is doing and to what.

Next we'll move the logic from **prepare_addresses** to new methods. The earlier example had two lines of code that performed two different operations, whose details are not important and should be hidden in a method.

```
1   class Address
2     attr_accessor :street, :zip
3
4     def initialize(street, zip)
5       @street = street
6       @zip = zip
7     end
8   end
9
10  address1 = Address.new("123 Street", 12345)
11  address2 = Address.new("321 Street", nil)
12
13  def prepare_addresses(addresses)
14    remove_nil_zips(addresses)
15    sort_by_zip(addresses)
16  end
17
18  def remove_nil_zips(addresses)
19    addresses.reject! { |address| address.zip.nil? }
20  end
21
```

```
22    def sort_by_zip(addresses)
23      addresses.sort_by { |address| address.zip }
24    end
25
26    prepare_addresses([address1, address2])
```

There are two new methods, **remove_nil_zips** and **sort_by_zip**, each performing a specific task on the address collection. We can improve these methods without affecting **prepare_addresses**. We removed the comments since the methods clearly give the intentions of the code, and the comments don't offer any more information than just reading the code.

The final change moves the code into a class, which will group the functionality together in a single container. We will remove code and simplify how it's used. Let's make that change:

```
1     class Address
2       attr_accessor :street, :zip
3
4       def initialize(street, zip)
5         @street = street
6         @zip = zip
7       end
8     end
9
10    class AddressCleaner
11      def initialize(addresses)
12        @addresses = addresses
13      end
14
15      def clean
16        remove_nil_zips
17        sort_by_zip
18      end
```

```
19
20     private
21
22     def remove_nil_zips
23       @addresses.reject! { |address| address.zip.nil? }
24     end
25
26     def sort_by_zip
27       @addresses.sort_by { |address| address.zip }
28     end
29   end
30
31   address1 = Address.new("123 Street", 12345)
32   address2 = Address.new("321 Street", nil)
33
34   address_cleaner = AddressCleaner.new([address1, address2])
35   addresses = address_cleaner.clean
```

We have introduced a class, **AddressCleaner**, which takes an array of addresses and provides a single method, **clean**. Also, we moved **remove_nil_zips** and **sort_by_zip** to private methods since we do not want them being used outside the class. The method name, **clean**, describes the task without providing unnecessary details. Knowing how we clean the addresses isn't important to the calling code or the reader, they only need to know they are getting clean addresses from the method. Since we encapsulate the clean logic, we can add more cleaning logic without updating the calling code.

We will stop there with our refactoring changes. Each small change we made got us closer to better code. In this chapter, we made these changes one after another, but that isn't necessary. Stopping anywhere along the refactoring process is okay. Any improvement leaves the code better than you found it. If making a large refactoring is intimidating, make a small one and come back later. Small improvements are better than none.

Single Responsibility Principle

It's tough to know if a method is only "doing one thing", since people might interpret that differently. Even if you have a handle on it, it's easy to convince yourself otherwise. Generic class names can give developers clearance to add methods that should otherwise be in a new more specific class. A mistake new Rails developers make is using a model class as a catchall for related logic.

Here is an example:

```
1  class User < ApplicationRecord
2    def trail_user?
3      self.trail_end_date <= Date.today
4    end
5  end
```

Here we have an ActiveRecord model class with a method that handles user licensing. The developer who wrote **trail_user?** related the method to a user, and decided it belonged in the **User** class. While **trail_user?** uses trail_end_date, which belongs to the **User** class, licensing is not specific to a user. The application might start licensing by user and later change so it's associated with a company. This is a common story for applications as they mature and try to reach different customer types.

On top of this, the **User** class already is responsible for retrieving data from the database and storing it in an object. Adding a method for licensing adds a role and breaks SRP (Single Responsibility Principle). After you violate the rule once, it becomes easier to do it again. Eventually, you will end up with a very large class that has many roles and thousands of lines of code. The class will become a problem because it's very hard to support and test.

If the licensing code doesn't belong in the **User** class, where does it belong? The answer is simple: a new class with the role of managing licenses.

```
1    class User < ApplicationRecord
2    end
3
4    class License
5      def initialize(user)
6        @user = user
7      end
8
9      def trail?
10       @user.trail_end_date <= Date.today
11     end
12   end
```

Our new class **License** takes an instance of **User** and exposes a single method, **trail?**. The new method checks to see if the user's trail end date is past the current date. If not, then we still consider it a trail license; otherwise, the trial license has expired.

The class **License** has a single role; it handles the details of how licensing works for the application. In its current form, we tie the licensing to the user. Since the method is separate from the User class, we can add new methods and even change licensing to use a company instead of a user without affecting code that uses the User class. We have more flexibility in testing. We can use an instance of the **User** class, or avoid the database call and create a mock of the user class. This flexibility can help speed up unit tests.

CHAPTER 7

Test-Driven Development (TDD)

Test-driven development is a scary topic for many new developers, but the concepts are simple. Once you get the hang of TDD, the benefits become clear. Your code will be simpler, cleaner, and easier to refactor. With TDD, we only write the code we need to write, and avoid adding unnecessary fluff. It will no longer be a scary prospect to make changes to your code. You have tests to verify that your changes won't break existing code. If something goes wrong, you'll know where the break occurred.

Our goal for this chapter is to create a **Calculator** class that has a single method. That method will return the sum of two values. This is the only requirement. How we implement the method is up to us. This represents day-to-day development. When working with a team, you will often receive work from non-technical people. It's your responsibility to decide how your code works. Unit tests will confirm your assumptions and will continue to work.

Start with Tests

The TDD method states we should create our tests first before writing any real code. We will follow this approach. We will create our own mini "testing framework." This is an exaggeration since the framework will only contain a single method to test equality. The concept is the same; a full-fledged testing framework provides more options to validate our code.

© Carleton DiLeo 2019
C. DiLeo, *Clean Ruby*, https://doi.org/10.1007/978-1-4842-5546-9_7

To start, create a class named **CalculatorTest** with a single private method named **equal?**. This method will test the equality of two values. If they are equal, the method will print the word **PASS** to the console; if not, it will print the word **FAIL**.

```
1    class CalculatorTest
2    private
3    # Test if two values are equal
4    def equal?(a, b)
5     if a == b
6       puts 'PASS'
7     else
8       puts 'FAIL'
9     end
10    end
11    end
```

Now, let's create the first test. At the beginning of the chapter, we stated the following: create a class with a method that returns the sum of two values. Our first test will test this requirement.

```
1    class CalculatorTest
2      def should_add_two_values()
3        # This is the value we expect to be returned by the add
         method expected = 5
4
5        calc = Calculator.new
6        # Call the add method with two values that equal 5
7        result = calc.add(3, 2)
8
```

```
 9      # Check if result equals the expected value
10      equal?(result, expected)
11    end
12
13    private
14    # Test if two values are equal
15    def equal?(a, b)
16     if a == b
17       puts 'PASS'
18     else
19       puts 'FAILS'
20     end
21    end
22    end
23
24    tests = CalculatorTest.new
25    tests.should_add_two_values
```

The first line of our test sets our expected value to 5. I chose the value at random, but we could use any number. Then we create an instance of our *future* **Calculator** class and call the **add()** method passing two values that should equal our expected value of 5. We defined what our Calculator class will look like. As we write more tests, we will make more decisions how we compose our code. The tests will become a checklist of features our code must complete.

We check to see if the result of the add method is equal to the expected value. If you run this code as is, it will fail because we haven't defined our **Calculator** class. Let's define that class now.

Implement Our Code

```
1   class Calculator
2     def add(a, b)
3       a + b # The most simple way to make our test pass
4     end
5   end
```

Our new **Calculator** class comprises a single method, **add**, that takes two values and returns the sum of those values. This is the simplest solution to get our test to pass. That is an important concept when following TDD; *only write the code required to make your test pass*. It helps us avoid the fluff we mentioned before and having code that isn't tested.

More Tests

If we run our code, we will see **PASS** displayed in our terminal. Now we have one test completed, we should consider other ways someone might use our code. What if someone tried to pass two nil values to our method? Let's create a test to see what happens.

```
1   # This method should be added to our CalculatorTest class
2   def should_add_two_nil_values
3     # We need to decide what we expect the result of nil +
        nil is expected = 0
4
5     calc = Calculator.new
6     result = calc.add(nil, nil)
7
8     equal?(result, expected)
9   end
```

```
10   ...
11   tests.should_add_two_nil_values
```

The second test is like the first test. We changed the expected value to 0, and the two values passed to the add method to **nil**. For the expected value, I decided I wanted the add method to return 0 if we pass it two **nil** values, but you might decide you want your method to return **nil**. These choices might be up to you, or you may need to ask the person who requested the feature. It's possible they might not have thought about it. You need to make sure your test validates your assumptions.

If you run our test, we would get the following error:

```
1   undefined method '+' for nil:NilClass (NoMethodError)
```

We've discovered it's not possible to add to nil values together. This means we need to change our method to handle **nil** values. A simple solution casts parameters to integers, regardless of type. For NilClass,[1] this will result in the value 0. So that means instead of *nil + nil*, we get *0 + 0* which equals 0.

```
1   class Calculator
2     def add(a, b)
3       a.to_i + b.to_i
4     end
5   end
```

If we rerun our tests, all should pass. We should continue this line of thinking until it satisfies us we have thought of all ways someone might use our code. If we want our code to be robust, then we need to think about how future developers might use it. By doing this, we can use our code knowing that if someone else makes changes, our tests will act as a warning alarm.

---

[1]https://ruby-doc.org/core-2.4.0/NilClass.html#method-i-to_i

TTD using other frameworks like Rspec[2] isn't much different from what we've done here. The concepts are the same; we have more ways to write our tests. Try not to get overwhelmed by the number of features available in your testing framework. It's more important we write tests than to find the best way to write them. Just like our production code, we can refactor tests.

Clean Tests

Unit tests are an important part of software development. Tests verify assumptions and protect against future breakage. It's important to give our tests the love and attention they deserve. If your tests are hard to read, other developers won't understand what you are testing. They will have difficulty finding gaps in your tests during pull request code reviews.[3] Changes to the test code will result in further problems. What is the difference between a good and bad test? Let's look at some examples.

```
1  class Calculator
2    def add(a, b)
3      a + b
4    end
5
6    def subtract(a, b)
7      a - b
8    end
9  end
```

---

[2]http://rspec.info/
[3]https://help.github.com/articles/about-pull-request-reviews/

The class has two methods, **add** and **subtract**. Now look an example of poorly written tests (I'm using Rspec[4]).

```
1   RSpec.describe Calculator do
2     it "returns added value" do
3       c = Calculator.new
4       expect(c.add(2,2)).to eq(4)
5     end
6
7     it "returns subtracted value" do
8       c = Calculator.new
9       expect(c.subtract(2,2)).to eq(4)
10    end
11  end
```

The Rspec file has two tests. First, we verify the functionality of the **add** method; then we check the **subtract** method. These tests have several problems.

1. Test descriptions are vague.

2. Not using Rspec features to simplify tests.

3. Unclear test expectations.

4. Difficult to understand how the test verifies the method it tests.

Now let's see an example of well-written tests. We should write several additional tests, but we will leave them out for simplicity.

```
1   RSpec.describe Calculator do
2     context '#add' do
3       it "returns sum of two values" do
4         expected = 4
```

---

[4]http://rspec.info/

```
5      actual = subject.add(2, 2)
6      expect(actual).to eq(expected)
7    end
8  end
9
10  context '#subtract' do
11    it "returns difference of two values" do
12      expected = 1
13      actual = subject.subtract(3, 2)
14      expect(actual).to eq(expected)
15    end
16  end
17 end
```

The test file has several changes that improve readability.

1. Rspec **context** groups relevant tests. We also append
   "#" to the method name to identify an instance
   method. If the method were a class method, we
   would append "::" to the method name.

2. Better descriptions for each test.

3. Explicitly declaring a variable for the expected and
   actual values.

4. Instead of creating the Calculator class manually, we
   use the implicitly defined subject.[5]

We should place additional tests for each method inside their
respective context. The improved structure and readability of the test code
makes it easier for other developers to review and contribute. Better test
coverage means fewer bugs, and that's always good.

---

[5]https://relishapp.com/rspec/rspec-core/v/3-7/docs/subject/
implicitly-defined-subject

AFTERWORD

Wrapping Up

Writing clean, beautiful code is a career-long pursuit for any developer. As you improve your code, you will find new and better ways to write code. There are so many approaches and methodologies for writing code. The concept of "clean code" is highly debated within any programming community.

It's easy to become overwhelmed trying to make your code perfect. Don't get stuck on finding the optimal technique. Remember that chasing dreams of perfect code can prevent you from finishing tasks or entire projects. A complete working application is much more valuable to a user than an incomplete application with perfect code.

Make informed decisions when you program. Use the tools you've learned in this book to make your code a little better each time you sit down to write it. Take a single idea and try focusing on it until it becomes second nature. Eventually, you will incorporate the idea without a thought.

Finally, keep up with changes to Ruby. Each new version introduces changes that will make your life easier. Take the time to learn the classes and methods available to you in the Ruby language. You will discover hidden tools that will surprise you.

Good luck on your journey; never stop learning.

© Carleton DiLeo 2019
C. DiLeo, *Clean Ruby*, https://doi.org/10.1007/978-1-4842-5546-9

Index

Printed in the United States
By Bookmasters